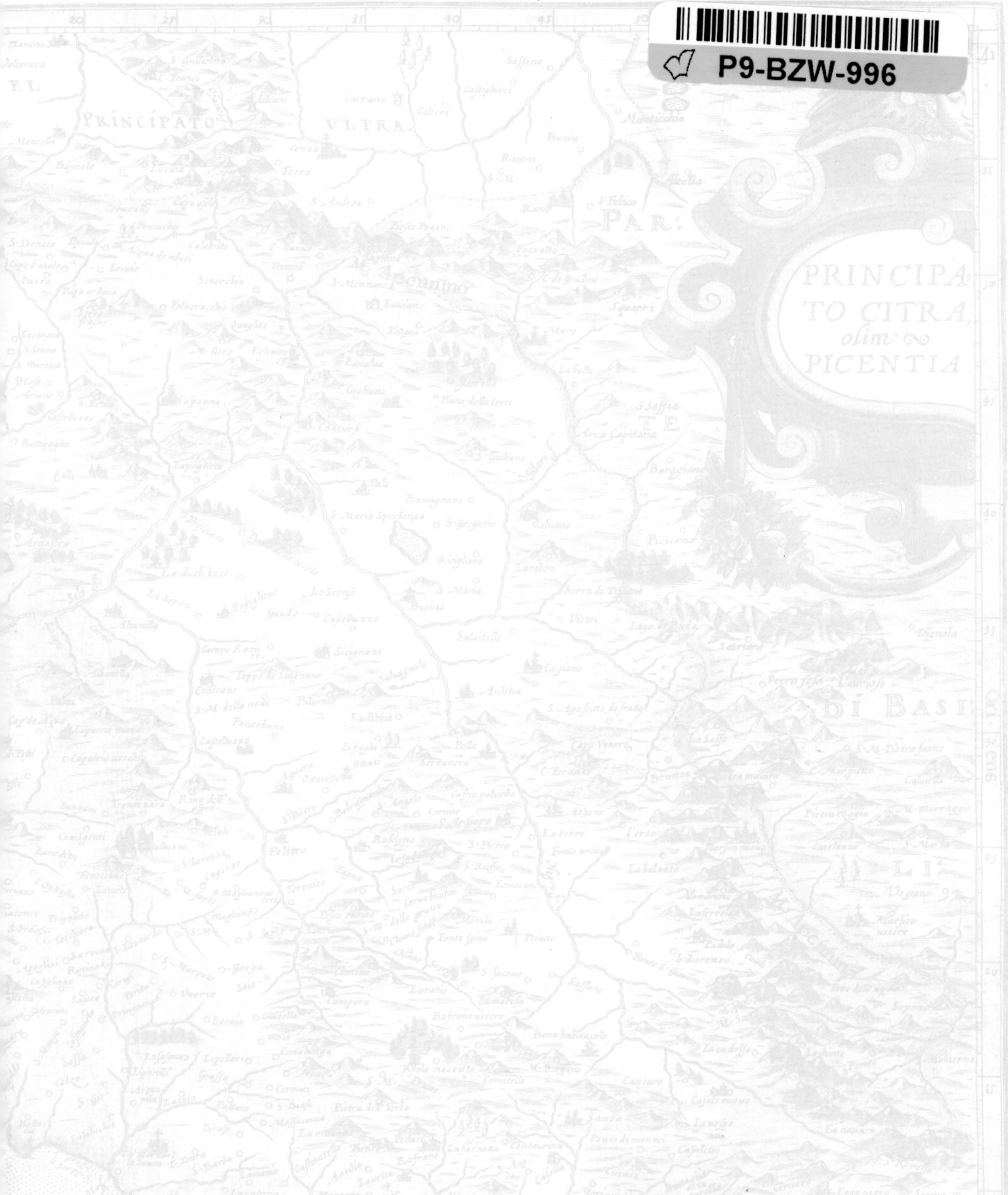

PRINCIPATO CITRA, olim PICENTIA
PRINCIPATO
VLTRA
PAR:
Apennino
DI BASI
LI
CATA
GOLFO DI POLICASTRO
Monticchio
Altella
Buisie
Rapone
S. Felice
Ruuo
Muro
La bella
S. Soffia
Arca Capitana
Barragiano
Piciernò
Vabiano
Larston
Serra de Trigono
Vitri
Lago de Buda
Satriano
Dignola
Caiano
Aulcha
Saluitelli
S. Maria
Busino
S. Gregorio
Romagnano
S. Maria Sporlonga
Pale
S. Giuliano
Coghiano
Lacaena
Capagna
Pontecagnano
Eboli
Altavilla
Albanella
Sicignano
Lo Scorpe
Castelluzzo
Caiano
Polla
Atheno
La torre
S. Pietro
Diano
S. Iacouo
Sassano
Sanza
Castelluzzo
Capaccio vecchio
Castellabate
Felitto
Lauriano
S. Brancato
Trecchina
S. Filippo
Lagonegro
Moliterno
T. la Scalella
T. Calamarescu
T. Infresco
T. lo Cernaro
T. le cuerne
Maratia Sup.
T. de Capriola
Policastro
Rofrano
Torre Orsaia
S. Seuerino
Padula
Casale nuovo
S. Lorenzo

For Gaia

Positano

THE VERTICAL CITY

Romolo Ercolino

NicolaLongobardiEditore

For all the people from Positano who are no longer with us, whose stories and first-hand accounts have helped to keep alive memory of the past and feelings of love towards our birthplace.
It is now up to the young people to preserve these nobles values because – as the Amalfi historian Matteo Camera put it long ago – "if one doesn't know how to read the past he obviously doesn't care about the present and still less about the future".

Publication of this book has been made possible thanks to:
- the cultural awareness of the City of Positano Administration and its Mayor, Domenico Marrone
- Lorenzo Cinque, President of the Tourism section of the Salerno Industrial Association
- the Provincial Tourist Board
- Benedetto Santangelo, Commissioner of the Positano Tourist Board
- the following associations: Positano Hoteliers, Posidonia, Franco di Franco, Posimuse, Positanoarte, Nova Cella, Selva, Gea
- the Positano agency of Deutsche Bank
and the numerous friends and tourism operators who offered their kindness and support.

Special thanks are due to Nicola Longobardi, my nephew Luigi Ercolino (www.positanoline.it) and Lorenzo Saprio for all their help, and for providing most of the photographs in the book.
Last but not least, heartfelt thanks go to my friends Salvatore Ferraro, who took care of the original Italian text editing, and to Angelo Pesce, who thoroughly revised and integrated it in preparation of this English edition.

Translations: Angelo Pesce and Stephen Spedding

First English edition
Curator and Editor: Angelo Pesce

© 2009   *Nicola Longobardi Editore*
            Via Napoli, 201 - 80053 Castellammare di Stabia (Na)
            telephone and telefax 0818721910
            email: nleditore@libero.it

ISBN 978-88-8090-293-5

More than a century since the publication of Errico Talamo's Monografia sulle città di Positano, *and fifty years since Giuseppe Vespoli's* Storia di Positano, *this study is only intended as a token of love and appreciation for my birthplace, as well as a guide for those who want to know more about Positano's history and treasures, its amazing artistic, natural and environmental heritage, its inhabitants. The book traces different routes through the town's history and culture in a bid to uncover our local heritage, which amply deserves to be better known, protected and valued because carelessness, ignorance and indifference on our part mean that, with the passage of time, it will gradually vanish – as it already does – along with the historical message it embodies. Hopefully more people will be prompted to study it as a result.*

I have tried to gather what little remains of the traces left by the thoughts and actions of people in the past, the visible and tangible signs of the relationship between people and their environment. I have included those remains which managed to survive man's destructive fury, as well as any faded and forgotten accounts of the distant and recent past of an old and new town. In this way people can rediscover their roots and their historic-cultural identity and thereby have a better understanding of the present as an integral and inseparable part of our collective memory, because – quoting Sepulveda – "those peoples who do not know their history properly, carry on making the same mistakes".

To readers interested in and fascinated by local history, I hope I have given an opportunity and a tool for understanding our culture better, the kind of reading which will stimulate and enhance their knowledge and love of the real Positano, with its history, its legends and its monuments, here re-assembled after patiently combing unusual routes, endless stone stairways and ancient footpaths, where fragments of the past, however faded and elusive they may be, can still be found. And it is these that help tie the knot in the very thin thread linking places to memory and past to present.

R. E.

5

Titbits of collective imagination

It is believed that the coastline from Reggio to Gaeta is perhaps the most delightful parts of Italy. Along it, quite close to Salerno, there is a stretch of land overlooking the sea – the inhabitants call it "la costa di Amalfi" – which is full of small cities, gardens and fountains.
(A fitting descriptive sentence by Giovanni Boccaccio in Decameron, Day 2, IV).

Positano is an enchanting place, about midway between Sorrento and Amalfi. One gets there running half the length of an extraordinary road carved into cliffsides rising straight from the shoreline. 'Divine Seacoast' is how they call the place the road runs through, and as a matter of fact it is hard to figure out a place more unearthly than this one.
All the famous roads contouring the Norwegian fjords, all the panoramic routes cutting across the Swiss mountains, beloved by travellers from everywhere, pale in comparison with this one, to the point of appearing trifle, to border on the risible.
On this Divine Seacoast I cast my anchor, and left it there to stay for a long time.
(The Russian journalist Michail Semenoff found, in the 1910s, these suitable words to describe the allure of Positano and its environment, the compelling attraction they exert on the unsuspecting passerby).

There were at that time a number of outsiders living in the small city: artists, hermits and eccentrics from all over the world (…) Each one of these mad foreigners – for they had created a sort of international community of eccentrics and hermits – claimed that his or her terrace was the most beautiful and it is true that each one proved better than the last one visited or, at least, appeared different, because it offered a new perspective on the sea.
(A tart, yet graceful comment on the 1930s expatriate colony in Positano by Stefan Andres, which can be read in his book Positano, Geschichten aus einer Stadt am Meer -München, 1957-, re-issued in Italian -Amalfi, 1991- with the title Positano, storia di una città sul mare).

Positano bites deep. It is a dream place that isn't quite real when you are there and becomes beckoningly real when you have gone. Its houses climb a hill so steep it would be a cliff except that stairs are cut in it. I believe that whereas most house foundations are vertical, in Positano they are horizontal. The small curving bay of unbelievably blue and green water lips gently on a beach of small pebbles. There is only one narrow street and it does not come down to the water. Everything else is stairs, some of them as steep as ladders. You do not walk to visit a friend. You either climb or slide.
(Such are some of the musings on Positano by John Steinbeck, in an article published in 1953 in the American magazine Harper's Bazaar).

SCROLLING THE PAGES OF HISTORY

Embraced and protected by the Monti Lattari and kissed by the Mediterranean, suspended between mountains and sea, Positano, thanks to its favourable geographical position and geomorphologic features, contains an amazing amount and diversity of beauty. Nature, landscape and architecture merge to produce the most wonderful scenes which are, for the most part, unspoilt and totally unique. Let us recall for a moment the majestic, imposing natural arch of Monte Gambera in the village of Montepertuso, which we will return to later. Among the countless natural arches in the world, this is claimed to be one of three, and the only one in Europe, where both the sun's and the moon's rays pass straight through at specific moments of the year.

The backbone of the Lattari range forms a perfect divide between the gulfs of Naples and Salerno. On its steeper Amalfi side, deep, narrow gorges are carved into it, where spring-fed streams flow, turning to gushing torrents in the winter season. The higher part is still covered in fairly dense vegetation left over from the original Mediterranean maquis with its beech, chestnut, oak and especially ilex trees (*Quercus ilex*),

Pages 6 and 7:
Landscape views

Page 8:
Via Monte

Page 9:
Vallone Porto

Previous page and below:
The pertuso opening of Mt. Gambera, produced by ancient karst activity

which in the 10th century still stretched as far as the sea. Then there are the typical bushes: rosemary, French lavender, broadleaved lavender (or spick, used by our grandmothers to make the laundry, or a bride's garments smell nice) woody spurge and true myrtle, a sacred plant and the symbol of peace for the ancient Mediterranean people. There is the spicy edible rocket and mastic formerly used by our fishermen to dye nets. Lots of other varieties of plants include the Mediterranean cypress and, along the coastline, the Aleppo pine.

Only Nature, with all her colours and scents, could have produced this enchanting garden. The landscape reveals the man-made changes that have shaped it from earliest times to make its soils more productive, with its characteristic terraces and dry-stone walls, made to contain the soil where vines and olives, the two plants that have always shaped and accompanied the lives of Mediterranean man, were grown. There are also carob and citrus trees, which have become special elements in the landscape, changing colours with the seasons.

The higher areas form an ideal habitat for a wide variety of fauna. Numerous birds of prey nest up there, including the peregrine falcon, kestrel and buzzard, as well as other bird species, both migratory and indigenous, whose song blends with the rustling of leaves.

Foxes, hedgehogs and, in the past, otters, were the kings of the Mediterranean maquis. In the spring the air is alive with numerous types of fluttering butterflies. The steep, craggy cliff-face is dotted with villas and houses, all with terraces and pleasant gardens constantly in bloom, reflected in the deep blue sea with countless shades of turquoise and cobalt. Where water channels and tiny narrow valleys occur, there are inlets and bays hiding beaches that can only be reached by boat. This means some peace and quiet can be enjoyed even during the summer months, when the tourist season is at its peak.

Positano is protected from the cold north winds by a girdle of mountains: to the north by S. Angelo a Tre Pizzi massif (the ancient Phoenician *Garul* and Roman *Gaurus*), at 1143m. the highest altitude attained by Monti Lattari, which is made up of the peaks of S. Angelo, S. Michele (formerly known as Monte Aureo[1]), and the Molare, joined from the west by Monte Conocchia, which means barrier; to the west by Monte Comune, known to the Phoenicians as *Saron*, and by S. Maria del Castello, where in ancient times a temple dedicated the goddess of the harvest existed; to the east by Monte Paipo, which means bald or stony.

To the southwest a view embracing the whole of the Gulf of Salerno from the nearby Vettica di Praiano, right round to Paestum

13

and Punta Licosa, can be enjoyed. Legend has it that the siren Leucosia, "the resplendent", who lived along with Parthenope and Ligea on the Sirenuse islands (now Li Galli) just offshore from Positano, was buried there and gave the place its name.

The western tip of the bay is formed by Punta Campanella[2] which, until the 16th century, was called *Promontorium Minervae* because there was an ancient temple to the goddess on a rocky salient. According to legend, the temple was built by Ulysses on his perilous return journey to Ithaca. Very close to Punta della Campanella stands the island of Capri which is nothing but an outlier of the Monti Lattari. When ancient sailors from Greece crossed the Bocche di Capri (Straits of Capri), the narrow passage dividing the island from the mainland, they used to pour a glass of their best wine into the water as a token of gratitude to the goddess for protecting them.

Thanks to its enviable position, propitious climate and charming landscapes, Positano truly deserves its titles of *Città Solare* or Sun Town and *Perla della divina Costiera* or Pearl of the Divine Coast.

It is impossible to say when the first settlements were established here. The earliest evidence of people inhabiting our land, where the combined action of sea and underground watercourses has formed scores of caves, dates back to the late Paleolithic period, attested as it is by some 350 artefacts, including a petroglyph of a deer or a horse, discovered in 1956, by A. M. Radmill and E. Tongiorgi of the Institute of Anthropology and Paleontology at the University of Pisa, in the Grotta La Porta[3], behind the namesake beach east of the Spiaggia Grande. These are currently housed in the Luigi Pigorini National Museum of Prehistory and Ethnography in Rome. Conversely,

there is no trace of the thirty-two archaeological finds that were left in the care of Positano Municipality.

No specific references to Positano exist in any ancient text nor in the *Tabula Peutingeriana*, hence it is possible that there was no settlement of note until the Augustan period. There are, however, numerous references to the Sirenuse islands, home to the Sirens, recorded in the works of Homer, Virgil, Ovid, Strabo, Lycophron of Chalcis and many other famous poets and scholars.

The legend of the Sirens, whose sweet singing and seductive charm cast a deadly spell on the sailors, still forms part of the collective memory. It takes us back to the time when the western Mediterranean was colonized, first by the Phoenicians, who certainly claimed possession of Li Galli islands and used them as a halting-place, and then by the Greeks. The name *gaulli*, which was what these islands were called until the late Middle Ages, most likely came from the word *gaulos*[4], the name given to the Phoenician trading ships.

Positano's origins, like those of the majority of places, are steeped in myth and legend. One of these says that it was founded by the Phoenician god of the sea Pesitan (the Greek god Poseidon) in honour of his favourite nymph, the younger of the Graces, the charming Pasitea[5]. It is not for nothing that the great historian Livy (59 BC - 17 AD) wrote: "It is to be conceded such kind of licence to ancient writers who, to ennoble the origin of cities, mixed the human with the divine".

Apart from various legends seemingly indicatimg the existence of a *pagus* (hamlet), it was the Roman Imperial Age which finally cast some light on the history and events in our land. Numerous patrician

Previous page:
Tomb of E. Savino and sarcophagus with Bacchus' legend, Church of the Rosary

Opposite:
Fresco from the Positano Roman villa (from *Le ville romane in Costiera amalfitana*)

Below:
Sea monster on a marble pluteus of the 11th-12th century, now above the entrance door to the campanile of the Assunta Church

villas were built along the coasts of our peninsula in that period, and in many instances their vestiges have miraculously survived the destructive forces of man and nature, and can still be admired aplenty. Two such villas were built on Li Galli islands and near Positano's main beach. Little remains of the former, but the one in Positano is almost completely buried under a layer of lapilli and ash, although many of its treasures have been plundered over the last few years. It is only recently that the part of the villa underlying the Oratory has been uncovered. This Roman villa, which can be dated back to the 1st century AD, was buried along with Herculaneum, Pompeii and Stabiae during the 79AD eruption of Vesuvius, known as the Plinian eruption. The famous archaeologist Matteo della Corte, who carried out in-depth studies into the etymology of Positano, maintains that the villa was built by one of Claudius Augustus' freedmen called *Posides*. Thus the name Positano would derive from the villa's name, *praedium* (holding, estate) *Posidetanum*.

In documents dating back to the 16th century, only the name Pasetano or Posetano can be found. The first variant, which is still used in all the local dialects, according to many scholars derives from the Greek *pas tanaos* (entirely precipitous), which is an apt description of our difficult terrain. The Greek etymology in the name Positano is not the only one in local place names, as we have seen. It is the survival of ancient names, passed down through the spoken language with only slight modification, along with the archaeological remains found in the area, that enables us to firmly fix the roots of an early settlement linked to the *praedia*, originating a wealth of ancient Roman place names in local topography.

The two Roman villas, a sarcophagus representing the Bacchus myth (poorly kept in the Rosario church in Piazza dei Mulini), a funerary base in the church at Montepertuso, some ash urns which were found and then, luckily, used as lavabos in local churches, even though they deserved a more dignified museum setting, numerous pieces

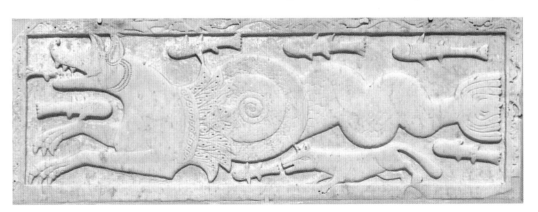

of columns scattered all over the town – all
of these testify to the presence of a settlement dating back to the 1st century AD.
This was a time when many Roman patricians, to be closer to the emperors Augustus
and Tiberius, who loved to escape to Capri,
chose the Campania coast to spend their
holiday and leisure time.

With the fall of the Roman Empire,
many upper class Romans fled to our hills to
escape the barbaric hordes. Later, with the
arrival of the Basilian monks, belonging to
the ancient order founded by S. Basilio and
already well established in other regions of
Southern Italy, the Positano Roman villa, or
what was left of it, became a refuge, and

an abbey was built on its ruins in honour of the martyr S. Vito[6]. Later, with the legendary arrival, at the beginning of the XIII century, of the icon of the Black Madonna from the Orient and its collocation in the main church, the abbey, by that time turned Benedictine, was also dedicated to the Madonna Assunta (Assumption), which is celebrated on 15 August.

The history of the abbey is intertwined with that of the agricultural landscape, because it was the Basilian monks who transformed its physical appearance – here as elsewhere – by creating terraces, which would enable them to increase the amount of usable agricultural land. The close network of religious and commercial relations developed between the various abbeys, which also acted as centres where family groups gathered, was fundamental to the rebuilding of local social and religious life and the conservation of the unity and culture of local folks. Such communities, focused on religion, formed the core of the hamlets that dotted the area, and later of the towns and villages.

The arrival of the Arabs, who settled along the Middle Eastern and North African coasts of the Mediterranean from the 7th century onwards, changed the already precarious political conditions and relations in many places – not only in Europe. The Mediterranean that until that point had acted as a unifying element for countries on its shore, now turned into a battlefield. Its coastline became a frontier to defend from the incursions of ever fiercer and more bloodthirsty Saracen pirates[7] who, taking advantage of the wars between the Longobards, Byzantines, Normans etc., managed to gain possession of Sicily, which they then governed for almost three centuries.

At the beginning of every favourable season these "sea devils", as the Saracens were referred to, made a series of quick raids on our coastlines spreading terror and death. Many coastal towns were deserted as a result in favour of higher-standing sites, which being less accessible, were also safer. After the final destruction of Paestum during the night of 23 June 916 in the hands of Saracens who had settled at Agropoli, some of the inhabitants who had managed to escape the bloodshed fled to Positano, where they asked the monks at the abbey for refuge and help. The monks gave them plots on the town's upper slopes, where they had a better chance of creating some agricultural land once they had chopped down the trees. They were housed in Laurito, in an area east of Montepertuso, thereafter christened Pestella (little Paestum) in memory of their lost hometown, and in Nocella – not Nocelle, as the highest and most isolated part of Positano is commonly called these days. The name Nocella derives in

Previous page:
Typical fishing tackle
Below:
Mt. S. Angelo a Tre Pizzi summit

fact from the Greek *neos kelos* through the Latin *nova cella*, which means new home or new refuge.

Montepertuso and Nocella gradually evolved into typical mountain villages whose natural defences provided refuge and safety for the people from the coast in times of danger.

At the end of the first millennium, with the influx of so many refugees, our steep hillsides started to be re-shaped and sculpted. They created the typical terracing with dry limestone walls (*macère*) carving out small flat areas with a thin layer of humus and planting vines and olives, which give the land its special character today. The historian Matteo Camera described this prodigious work, which spanned centuries, in the following terms: "the tireless hand of Man, forcing Nature, has found here a way to bend the bare rocky crags and stony valleys to the requirements of agriculture[8]".

Positano, embraced by rough mountains which kept it isolated from main communication routes until the last century, and with its soil not productive enough to allow for the development of agriculture, always depended on its essential sea-links for survival. The meagre fishing resources alternated, as still do today – except in very few cases – with those of the land.

"On the other hand, a fishing community was always set up near coastal mountains not only because of the forests but also because of the shelter they offered, especially on the north shores of the Mediterranean. These mountains descend naturally towards the sea (…) and the tempting liquid planar surface was often the best, or maybe the only, route between one coastal point and another. A link was thus forged between the fishing communities and the mountain economies. They complemented and strengthened each other[9]".

During the Dukedom of Amalfi (X-XII century), which included Positano, outbound ships sailed the Mediterranean routes and especially those headed for Liguria, Provence and Cataluña. 112-oar and 70-oar galleons, along with other smaller boats for transporting merchandise or for hunting down pirates, were built in our shipyards. Privateers from Positano, as in other towns in the Dukedom of Amalfi, carried out this warlike activity under a royal licence.

The leading shipyard owners of the time were the Buonocores, the Celentanos, the Cimminos, the Mirellis from Nocella village, the Talamos and many others.

It is said that a man from Positano, by the name Flavio Gioia according to legend, perfected the art of the magnetic needle[10]. He placed it over the wind rose in a wooden box (*bossolo*) whence the Italian name for compass, *bussola*.

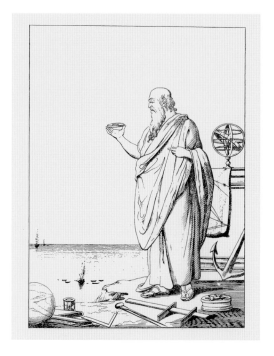

ALLA MEMORIA
SEI VOLTE SECOLARE
DEL SUO CONCITTADINO
GLORIA IMMORTALE
DI LEI E D'ITALIA
FLAVIO GIOJA
LA RISORGENTE POSITANO ANTICA
CON ENTUSIASMO
DI GRATITUDINE E DI SPERANZA
AGOSTO MDCDII

Previous page:
Lemons of the *sfusato amalfitano* variety

Below:
Valle dei Mulini in the 1920s

This is the outstanding contribution our town made to mankind, because it enabled people to travel new routes and discover new worlds much more safely. Further evidence of this close relationship with the sea is seen in the number of churches scattered about our territory, erected by shipyard owners and sailors and almost always dedicated to the Apostles who had been fishermen. Only the memory of most of these chapels remains now but, until the last century, at least a score were still standing.

The Amalfi Dukedom always enjoyed good trade links and relations with the Arab nations that influenced our land more than we can imagine: coffee was introduced to us because of them, as well as the cultivation of carob trees, eggplants, sugar cane, peaches and apricots. What proved even more important was that they started cultivating citrus fruits again. These were already popular in the Roman period, especially lemons, the symbol of life. Lemons have come to characterize our agricultural landscape and have been one of the main sources of wealth for centuries. Pasta making, which originated in Sicily in the XI century, quickly spread, as did other skills acquired from the Arabs,

to mainland Italy. We also have to thank our trade links with the Arab world for the rice cultivation in Sicily, Calabria and Spain, as well as the use of horizontal-slatted water mills, known as Arab mills, which had been in use for centuries in the East[11].

Historians consider the harnessing of water power as the first step toward technological change, which, centuries later, would lead to the Industrial Revolution.

Apart from this kind of mill, widely used on the Amalfi coast until the last century, we also learnt from the Arabs how to make paper. The art spread through Spain, Palermo and Amalfi to the rest of Europe, and this enabled people to learn about Arab culture and increased interest in classical culture.

Amalfi and Tramonti still have small factories producing hand-made paper with traditional methods.

Contact with the Arab world left its mark on culture as well. Civil, religious and military architecture were all influenced: cross- and barrel- vaults, crossed arches (upon which Gothic arches are based) as well as the tiles and ceramics which are still produced in local factories, are all subconscious reminders of our past relationship with the Arab world.

Salerno Medical School, the first Italian school to gain international recognition, and one which also accepted women as students, taught the principles of Greek, Roman, Hebrew and Arab medicine and there were always on the staff teachers from a variety of ethnical groups. Trocta, who was better known as Trotula, was famous for her research into women's ailments.

The defeat of Southern Italy at the hands of the Normans in the XII century signalled the end of the Dukedom of Amalfi and,

albeit slowly, the gradual decline of other towns associated with it.

With the arrival of the Angevins and after the bloody revolt of the "Sicilian Vespers" in 1282, the number of pirate attacks increased. This was also the fault of the Aragonese who had rushed to Sicily's aid, destroying whole coastal areas and causing havoc in the ports, the main access for food supplies. To try and protect the defenceless populations from these continued attacks, a series of lookout towers and forts were built along the entire coast. Each one could communicate with the next, using smoke signals during the day and fires at night. Both served to warn citizens of the approach of enemy galleys[12] so they could flee to safety or prepare to defend themselves[13].

To get this impressive defence system up and running, the Royal Treasury had to rely on private financing. The sponsors were appointed *castellani* or *torrieri* (castle or tower masters) in exchange.

Once the king Robert of Anjou passed the edict in 1332, the first tower was built on Li Galli. Pasquale Celentano[14] from Positano was in charge of its construction, and he also headed the projects on the other two islands, Briganti and Rotonda. The remains of these forts can still be seen on Briganti island.

We do not know who built the other towers along the Positano coast, namely the Sponda tower, which was restored by the Pattison - Gaetani family in the 1920s, and is the only one to preserve its original military structure; the Trasino (meaning between two inlets or beaches) tower, whose name has changed over the years to Trasita, erected to defend the Sirene and Fornillo beaches, and rebuilt in the 1950s; the Fornillo or Jermano tower, which was rebuilt in

the 1920s by the Swiss poet and dramatist Gilbert Clavel, and the five towers which lie inland. References to a Rienzo tower behind the Arienzo beach[15] exist, but only the memory of its location has survived.

In 1343 a devastating, completely unexpected tidal wave struck the coast. What caused it was never clear but it affected the whole of the Campania coastline and killed many people. The rebound wave finished the job off. There were more than three hundred deaths, and the damage caused was enormous. Queen Jean I of Anjou decreed that the people of Positano did not have to pay their taxes for twenty years to help them recover from this tragedy.

In 1440 Positano was pillaged by brigands from Cilento and by Saracen pirates.

The inhabitants fled to the mountains and the monks from the local abbey decided to transfer to Cava de' Terreni as they felt far too exposed to permanent danger in Positano.

In 1441, Pope Paul II entrusted the church and monastery to a Commendatory Abbot (as a rule, a member of the high clergy) who relieved them of most of their treasures. A few columns in African breccia marble were sold to the Sisters of the SS. Trinità church in Naples, and an ancient green breccia altar and porphyry font were given to the Cathedral in Amalfi in exchange for two cast-iron lions. These were placed on either side of the steps leading to the beach, and were intended as decoration for a fountain, which was never built. There is no record of many other artefacts. When

Franco Sarandrea inc.

Positano
Scorcio de "Li Galli" dalla Torre di Fornillo

the Turks took Constantinople on 29 May, 1453[16], the consequences for the West were dreadful. Southern Italy was particularly affected because of its geographical proximity and vulnerable position to attack from the Muslim world. The first tragic indications of what this might imply were seen during the siege and subsequent capture of Otranto, the easternmost town in Italy, on 8 August 1480. The siege lasted only eight days and, once Otranto had surrendered, 800 of its inhabitants were beheaded[17] because they refused to renounce their faith.

Until the battle of Lepanto in May 1571[18], the Mediterranean was the uncontested domain of bloodthirsty Turkish pirates led by Khayr al-Din Khidher, known as Redbeard, who had the gall to advance as far as the mouth of the Tiber river on 1 August 1534. Other infamous pirates were known as and Dragut, to name but a few. Their attacks on ships and coastal towns became more and more frequent, and they hijacked boats and kidnapped people, most of them bound to become their slaves and concubines.

The alliance between the King of France, François I, who was constantly at war with Emperor Carlos V of Spain and the Ottoman Porte, favoured the expansion of the Ottoman war. This led to the construction of a new line of defence along the coast, although the situation out at sea remained critical as the only ships to oppose the Muslim advance were fleets from Venice, Genoa, Pisa and the Knights of Malta.

New towers, of a different shape and size, were built, each within sight of the next and equipped with firearms, which had come to Italy along with Charles VIII King of France.

A drawing detailing the outline of the Amalfi Coast which was done in 1637 by the German cartographer Luc Holste, now kept in the Vatican library, gives a clear idea of how many towers there were to protect it. No cannons were ever fired from a large number of these towers, but they were often instrumental in dissuading enemy attacks, to the point that the Venetian Ambassador at the Court of Naples tried to persuade Venice to adopt the same defence system because it had proved so effective.

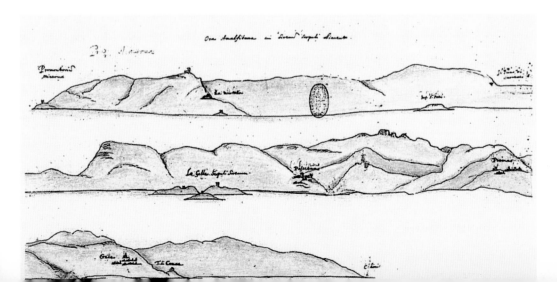

The Gold Mountain

On 18 August 1696, Positano freed itself of its feudal serfdom status by paying as much as 12.993 ducats to the State coffers. Economy and trade flourished and a period of prosperity followed. In 1705 there were 6 transport ships, 8 rowing boats, 8 hire boats, 10 fishing boats and 10 passenger boats. In 1724 there were 4 tartans, 24 large cargo boats, 14 large wooden rowing boats called *gozzi* and three fishing boats[19]. This increase in trade meant that the town got rich, earning the sobriquet "the gold mountain".

Nearly a century later, Positano was thus described: "no other town in the Kingdom has become so wealthy through its maritime trade[20]".

This had Gamelin – the French consul in Palermo – a bit worried, as he included the following sentence in a report[21] dated 17 August 1786: "…Moreover, there exists another people, which in spite of being very small and almost unknown, can't keep us from expressing our prejudice regarding its commerce with Sicily. The Positano people, inhabiting the Amalfi Coast, not far from Naples (a people always industrious which fathered the famous Flavio Gioia, inventor of the compass), is overly laborious, full of rectitude and of the knowledge necessary to navigation and related traffics. Organized in several companies headed by intelligent patrons and agents, it handles alone, with its feluccas, over a third of the import trade of Sicily, to the point that Sicilians and Genoans have often given them trouble. But the Naples Court has at all times decided in favour of the activity of this people, which has always been protected, obtaining the preservation of the remarkable privileges it nonchalantly enjoys in this Nation".

It was the sailors' custom to fire a cannon salvo as they left and then again on their safe return. The imported cargo was unloaded at the far end of the beach called *'o Cunto*. Over time this changed to *L'Incanto* (The Spell). 20% of profits went to the Church and the money was used to renovate or rebuild the places of worship. Private individuals built themselves some splendid houses in and around the town, which can still be admired today. They include the Palazzo Murat Hotel, which was built on the ruins of the old Benedictine abbey, Le Sirenuse Hotel, Villa Orseola, (formerly Villa Margherita), thus renamed by the antiquarian Raimondo Orselli who bought it in the 1950s, the other villas along Via S. Croce, Villa Stella Romana, as well as many more.

Some of these villas were still under construction or not yet complete when the French Revolution and subsequent occupation of the Kingdom of Naples came about, and they remained unfinished.

When Positano declared its allegiance to the ideal of liberty propagated by the French Revolution, and soon afterwards to the Napoleonic troops that had brought into submission the Kingdom of Naples, it found itself at odds with many of the neighbouring towns, especially Cetara, as they had remained faithful to the Bourbons.

Once Bonaparte had gained full possession (1806-1815) of the Kingdom of Naples and the English had occupied the island of Capri, Positano, as well as the Amalfi and Sorrento coasts, were attacked by part of the British fleet moored off Capri. The event was thus recorded by a contemporary newspaper, *Il Monitore delle Due Sicilie*, no. 220, with the dateline *Positano, 12 October 1811*:

49

POSITANO (PRINCIPATO CITERIORE) 12 OCTOBER 1811

"The day before yesterday we were witnesses to a spectacle which proved glorious not only because of the way the provincial guards from our town and nearby Conca reacted, but also the people of both places. A large convoy of ships arrived from Calabria, headed by the frigate captain Mr Barbera. Some of these ships were headed for Salerno but others were blown by the winds towards the port of Positano. An English frigate, five lance-ships and three cannon boats had been watching how the convoy split up. They sailed into our waters to try and take possession of the boats still anchored on our shores. Their ceaseless gunfire overpowered the cannon fire from the small battery on our boats. The enemy did everything within its power to take control of the convoy. They probably knew that the ships were carrying timber that would be used to build His Majesty's Navy vessels, but this made our men fight all the harder to save it. The firing from the fort stopped, and the enemy sent five armed lance-ships and three cannons to finish the job. Though they were covered by the frigate, which continued to fire all the time, our fusiliers managed to head them off and they were forced to turn round and retreat with many dead and injured sailors aboard. Annoyed at such unexpected resistance, the ships opened fire against the houses. This move was designed to scare the inhabitants and make them more amenable to the parliamentarian who, soon afterwards, came to ask for the ships and the building material to be handed over. If Positano failed to do this, they threatened to destroy the place. The enemy strategy did not have the desired effect: it simply made the whole population indignant. Mr Ettore, Commander of a detachment of Royal Corso [Corsican] Regiment posted at Positano, and Mr Alberto Cito, one of the town's magistrates, gave the parliamentarian a brave and decisive answer, and invited him to leave. The gunfire recommenced. Once it stopped, the parliamentarian returned, issuing new threats. The people said they would prefer to perish under the rubble of their houses rather than hand over one plank of timber from the ships. Their answer, which bore all the firmness real courage can bestow, persuaded the enemy that their efforts were in vain and they decided to back off. The population showed great consistency and courage on this occasion. The enemy cannons had set the alarm bells ringing in neighbouring villages and they quickly sent reinforcements to help. The detachment of Royal Corso Regiment mentioned above along with the legionnaires from Positano, Conca and neighbouring towns, customs officers and any other people who knew how to use firearms, fought valiantly. The enemy had two hundred men on board. The fighting lasted eight hours. None of our men lost their lives in the battle but two unfortunate women were caught in the firing line when the enemy gunned the houses".

POSETANO

Vista di
POSETANO
sul Mar Tirreno.

1. S.M. Asunta - 2. Torre Saracena - 3. Montepertuso - 4. M. Comune - 5. M. S. Angelo a Tre Pizzi - 6. Arco Naturale - 7. Torre a Mare - 8. C. Sottile.

On 9 September, 1806 Gaetano Gallo from Praiano, a privateer who was faithful to the Bourbon cause and to the money the English forces occupying Capri could offer, tried to land in Positano but without success.

"One hundred men led by Gaetano Gallo, known as *the deaf of Praiano*, and by Antonio Gambardella, landed their ships and started their attack at 9am. There were four cannon ships, which fired incessantly, to help them. But when a hundred men arrived from Salerno, and joined forces with the small Positano garrison, they quickly forced the enemy back onto their boats, leaving five men dead and five prisoners behind. And there were about thirty more dead on board (…) Peace was restored[22]".

Many of Positano's original inhabitants had, for business reasons, moved to other towns either within or outside the Kingdom. With the Restoration after the defeat of Napoleon, the idea that war was imminent made many of them come back and collect their families. The negative consequences of the war were that Positano lost most of her inhabitants and wealth.

These places were so difficult to get to. There was no access by land "unless you count the treacherous overgrown footpaths across the steep hostile mountains[23]". This meant that the foreign scholars and artists who had started to travel around the Kingdom of the Two Sicilies from the 18th century onwards, never went to Positano. There are more references to Li Galli isles than there are to Positano in accounts of the Amalfi coast. Only the more adventurous travellers found their way there. These included the French painter Marc Girardet who arrived in Italy at the end of the 18th century, maybe following the French troops, and painted what would become the first of many views of Positano, that is unless we count Pacichelli's engraving (reproduced above) dated to the beginning of the 18th century.

After the Kingdom of Naples was annexed by the Piedmontese, the Monti Lattari people were also attacked by groups of brigands led by the likes of *Cicione* and *Scorticaciuccio*. These attacks increased because there were so many Bourbon soldiers around, who felt morally justified because they preferred to stay loyal to their king rather than serve the new Savoy rulers. The Piedmontese army also played a role because they behaved like a subjugating rather than a unifying force.

The recession, which followed the unification of Italy, led to mass emigration. Many of Positano inhabitants, along with thousands of other southern Italians, were compelled to seek fortune and freedom abroad, especially in the USA. Positano had a population of 2761 in 1861. Within a few years this had gone down to 1710, a third less. When people heard how the first emigrants had settled abroad and were managing to provide for their families, they decided to follow their example, and whole areas of the town practically emptied. The Liparlati area was dubbed "the dead city" from then on. When the coastal road from Vietri sul Mare to Meta di Sorrento (the State Road 163 of today) was finished in the second half of the XIX century, it signalled the end of Positano isolation. Until then, access had only been by sea or along the ancient mountain "Pathway of the Gods" which has from time immemorial linked the two sides of the Sorrento peninsula.

The Twentieth Century

At the beginning of the 20th century, tourism started to make its first unassuming appearance in Positano. The town became a refuge for Italian artists including Vincenzo Caprile, a student at the Morelli school, who, for almost half a century, alternated between Naples, Venice and Positano, where he had an apartment in the Fornillo villa. How much he loved Positano is attested by the number of pictures he did of the beaches, daily life and architecture: "the artist whose brush conveyed the grandeur of the patrician marble houses on the Canal Grande, was also able to convey the humble freshness of the fishermen's cottages in Positano[24]".

He painted the Madonna Assunta in heaven, and the portrait of Clemente Savino, the owner of the house that became the Covo dei Saraceni Hotel, where the painting can still be admired. He also did the portrait of Angelina de Ruggiero. Franco Mancini, known as *the Lord* because of his elegance, painted what were then the ruins of the Fornillo tower. When these works became famous throughout the world, our town became a haven and refuge for a fairly large colony of foreign artists and writers. By choosing to make Positano their home, more and more people grew to know and appreciate Positano on account of the success of their work. One of the first people to fall in love with our town was the

Swiss writer and dramatist Gilbert Clavel. He was responsible for rebuilding the old Aragonese guard tower in its current pentagonal form[25]. He also renovated the Fornillo tower which he bought on 2 February 1909 from the Amendola family of Amalfi. Next was the Russian writer Michail Semenoff who bought and renovated the Arienzo mill. In 1917 Fortunato Depero arrived as a guest of Clavel and did the interior design for the tower. Semenoff also had as guests Igor Stravinskij, Pablo Picasso, Jean Cocteau and Sergej Pavlovic Diaghilev with his Russian Ballet company. Léonide Massine, who was already the company's star, was bewitched by Li Galli isles and, with Semenoff's help, bought them to set up an international dance school and a haven for young dancers.

On one occasion, when Gilbert Clavel asked Diaghilev what he thought of Positano, he answered: "It's the single example in the world of a vertical town".

Mention should also be made of the Swiss biologist Octo Bauer who built a series of stone ponds in the upper part of Vallone Porto to do research into amphibians.

After the fall of the Austro-Hungarian and Prussian Empires, and the Bolshevik revolution, many European artists and writers followed in Gilbert Clavel and Michail Semenoff's footsteps. Positano, which was still practically unknown and well outside the normal tourist circuit, became a haven

for artists who depicted its charm and ever-changing beauty in scenes of rare fascination. Amongst the first to arrive was Anita Rée, who did the famous portrait of Teresina Apuzzo, now in the Pinacoteca di Brera of Milan, and Maurits Cornelis Escher who stayed in Positano and other towns on the coast on several occasions between 1931 and 1935, paintings lots of rural landscapes and their spontaneous architecture, including "Vecchia casa a Positano" in 1934.

This colony of foreigners gradually grew, especially after the infamous Race Laws were passed in Germany, which forced many Jews and intellectuals who refused the Nazi ideology to flee to more hospitable countries. A document detailing the movement of foreigners in Positano from 1937 to 1940 reveals the yearly presence, on average, of about 13,000 foreigners, 70 of whom were referred to in bureaucratic jargon as "internees".

It is worth stopping to reflect for a moment on this phenomenon of forced emigration as a result of events in Russia and Germany, and ask what made our little town of Positano the chosen safe haven for so many foreign exiles.

Some people have said that it was because there was plenty of cheap housing on the market after so many of the inhabitants had emigrated to the States, the low cost of

living and the good wine. This, however, seems a rather shallow explanation, which bears little relation to the period in question. There were plenty of other towns that satisfied those criteria and offered even more, but immigrants did not choose them. The truth lies elsewhere.

Until a few years ago, Positano was isolated from the rest of the world, and, in many ways, still is today. Our only guests were painters and writers who were attracted not only by the beauty of the landscape, the mild climate and the peace and quiet, but also by the way local people treated them. Greek roots made them place great importance on hospitality and their particular brand of non-interfering hospitality meant that the foreign guests were offered kindness and friendship. Everything was done to make them feel at home – with no distinction of race, religion or creed – and part of a big family they could count on

in times of need. This was why many foreigners, after drifting around other coastal towns, maybe on the advice of people who had already settled here, preferred to stay in Positano. The long list includes the Polish lady Emilia Szenwic, who bought the Stella Romana villa and set up a literary circle there; the Russian Painter Ivan Zagoruiko, better known as *don Giovanni*, who came to Positano in 1930, and stayed here until his death in a Salerno hospital in 1964; Ilse von Knorring and her fellow countrywoman, the architect Anna Palme, a teacher at the Faculty of Architecture in Copenhagen, who dwelt here for long periods; the painter and master *tapissier* Martin Wolff who came in 1933 with his wife Mathilde Levy and their son Werner. On the 1936 population census, the Wolff family were registered as residents in Liparlati. Here the artist used an old loom – belonging to the last of the Positano weavers, Teresa Cinque – to

weave his tapestries, painting them with vegetable colours he made from berries and plants he found in the mountains. Wolff would often walk around with a basket to collect the various plants and this earned him the nickname *il signore col panariello* (the gentleman with the little pannier).

In 1942 the Wolff family were taken to the concentration camp at S. Lorenzo Nuovo, in Viterbo. They were deported by the Germans in 1943 and they all died at Auschwitz. Another elderly German Jew, Junker, and Mrs. Sachs who was also German and lived in Fornillo, left Positano in tears, convinced that they would never return. They did, in fact, perish in one of the Nazi death camps.

Another Jew, Robert Pariser, warned of his imminent arrest, fled Positano leaving all his belongings behind so as to throw the police off the scent. He managed to reach America, where he died in 1970.

Alberto Adler came to Positano with his wife and two sons in July 1936 and they were deported to Tuscania in the province of Viterbo in 1942. We should also remember Anita Brandt, Ilse Bondy and Rajzla Szlumien, who married the Positano painter, sculptor, writer and musician Raffaele Bella. The psycho-biologist Eduard Ghillausen[26], known to everyone as *don Eduardo, the Positano philosopher*, arrived on 19 March 1926. In Germany he was a student of prof. Grunow at the "Bauhaus Academy" in Weimar, before the Nazi regime closed it in 1934.

Other artists followed. There was Kurt Craemer, who first lived in a house on the beach where the Covo dei Saraceni Hotel stands now, and then in Fornillo; Karli

Sohn-Rethel and Bruno Marquardt, who arrived in the 1930s; the sculptress Brunhilde Damir Kind; the Jewish painter Paula Bärenfänger, who, although suffering from a degenerative paralysing disease painted what she could see from her bed; Irene Kowaliska, Polish, who reached Italy before Hitler came to power and worked for a long time with the German artists Riccardo Dolker[27], Margherita Hannaschy, Lisel Oppel and Gunther Studemann. This group, along with Max Melamerson, had been in Vietri since 1923 and had revolutionized the traditional methods for Vietri ceramics.

The writer Armin Teophil Wegner, who had witnessed and subsequently recorded the Armenian genocide at the hands of the Turks, was arrested by the Gestapo and exiled from Germany for writing to Hitler and asking him not to persecute the Jews. He fled to Positano with his wife, the writer Lola Landau, and their two children. We do not know much about their life. His wife emigrated with the two children to Palestine where she took an active part in the struggle to establish the new State of Israel.

Wegner stayed in Positano with his friend Irene Kowaliska, encountered years before in Berlin, and had a son with her. In April 1944 they both appear on the list of people helped by the Ente Comunale di Assistenza or local Council of Welfare. Kowaliska stayed in Positano until the late 1950s and, with her famous fabric designs, along with Countess Eva de Ruggiero, helped to establish the trendy Positano fashion.

The writer Stefan Andres, who was expelled by the Franco regime in Spain, moved to Positano in 1936 and stayed until the end of the 1950s. As a German citizen, he enjoyed privileges denied other refugees.

The Azerbaijan writer and journalist Lev Abramovic Nussimbaum, better known as Essad Bey, was born in Baku or, as he loved to say, on a train travelling between Europe and Asia, on 20 October 1905[28]. He came to Positano in the summer of 1938 – maybe already suffering from Reynaud's syndrome. He rented a house from Count Alfredo Pattison, who later, along with other locals, helped support him during difficult periods. He died of an excruciating illness on 27

August 1942. He was just 37 years old, and the only Muslim who received burial in our cemetery.

On 5 May 1942, only a few months before his death, he was in terrible pain because the morphine he so desperately needed had become unavailable to him. He wrote to the local Mayor in broken Italian begging for help.

His fiction works include *Alì and Nina, Twelve Caucasians, The Girl of the Golden Horn*, the non-fiction writings *Oil and Blood in the East* and *Allah ist Gross*, as well as biographic essays on Muhammad, Lenin and Stalin. He was ahead of his time, dealing, from the perspective of his Euro-Asian dual personality and culture, with issues that are still topical today.

His short but fruitful life, full of adventure and travail, saw him constantly fleeing the totalitarian regimes responsible for so much bloodshed in Europe in the first half of the 20th century. All his travelling made him change religion. Born into a Jewish family, he converted to Islam during his stay in Turkey and became Essad Bey (another pen-name he used was Kurban Said). Armin Teophil Wegner, who did not like him very much, maybe because he had renounced his family's faith, made this damning statement about him: "He enjoyed playing a comedian with himself and everyone else, right until the end."

After World War 2, lots of people tried to find out more about his real origins and controversial personality but, as always in such cases, the whole truth hardly emerged. The people of Positano never differentiated between the visitors and never judged their behaviour, political or religious choices because they were based on circumstances that were far from favourable at the time[29].

Other Russian artists who fled the Bolshevik regime included Grigorij Oscheroff, Aleksej Vladimirovic, Issupoff Aleksej David, Marussia Burljuk and Vasilij Nikolaevic Necitailov, better known as *don Basilio*, two of whose paintings hang in the Assunta church. Italian painters included Massimo Campigli, Ettore Pignone del Carretto, Angelo Landi di Salò and Celestino Petrone. There were so many artists who sought refuge from cruel totalitarian regimes or wars. This author hopes to able to write another book about them and all the others whose names are not mentioned here.

During WW2, Positano did not suffer massive blows from the tragedy which swept across Europe, but it paid all the same a high price in terms of lives lost in the fighting. Amongst those killed we should remember Luigi Cinque, shot by German troops in Naples during the four-day insurrection at the end of September 1943, in spite of the fact that he was a member of the Red Cross.

Positano provided the backdrop for some major war episodes. The English submarine *Safari*, which was hiding off Li Galli isles, ambushed the *Salemi* and *Val Savoia* merchant ships on 2 February 1943, at 14.50hrs and sank them both. This sad occasion provided further proof of Positano solidarity. When the submarine cannon was still firing at the *Salemi* because she was taking time to go under, local fisherman ignored the danger and took to their boats to try and rescue the sailors in the water. They took them on board and gave them water. Thanks to this action, only five people lost their lives that day.

Previous page:
Via della Teglia, by Nora Pattison

Opposite:
Portrait of J. Alfred Pattison, by Grigorij Oscheroff

Below:
Fontana Nuova

During the fighting, a torpedo, which had either missed its target or been deliberately fired at the Fornillo tower which housed a military barracks, hit the *Mamma e Figlio* (Mother and Son *faraglioni* or rocky stacks) near the tower, destroying most of the former. Stretching things a bit, local religious feeling interpreted this event as symbolic of the maternal love the Madonna of Positano showed her Son and the sentinels in the tower. In the early 1950s, an exceptionally rough sea completely destroyed what was left of both outcrops anyway.

After 8 September 1943 – the day when the "Armistice" between Italy and the Allied Forces was announced – there was another event which had tragic consequences. The Anglo-American Forces landed in the Gulf of Salerno in the early hours of 9 September and in due time a company of US Rangers, landed at Maiori, made their way to Positano.

To head off a German counter-offensive, they blew up the two road bridges, the Pantanelli and the new Fontana[30] at either end of the town. During the ensuing clashes, a German tank reversed through the barrier at the side of the road and plunged one hundred metres into the sea. The four casualties, initially buried in the Positano cemetery, were exhumed and moved to Montecassino German War Cemetery after the war. Once the bridges had gone, Positano was isolated and almost without provisions for a few months. It was only when the war started to go in the Allies' favour that communications were restored in the shape of two steel-and-planks Bailey bridges.

For the remainder of the war in Italy, Positano was a Rest Camp for the Allied troops, especially the British after the battle of Cassino. The American General Mark W. Clark, commander of the Fifth Army, also stayed here for a short time.

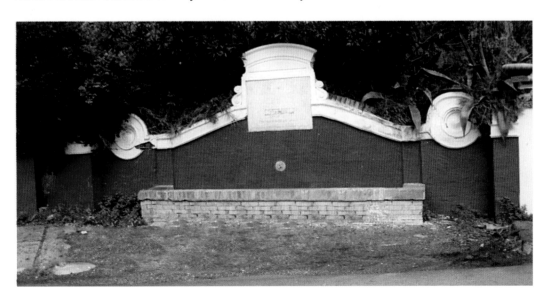

With the arrival of the Allies, the first tea-rooms and restaurants started opening up; a novelty in our town. Many people who stayed in Positano during that period came back once the war was over to appreciate its beauty and charm in peacetime. These included General Sir William D. Morgan[31], who was awarded honorary citizenship in recognition of his contribution to the town. It was thanks to him that Positano got its first aqueduct.

As times and fortunes changed, the number of tourists who were attracted by the climate and local amenities increased, and made Positano realize that her true vocation lay in tourism. A high-quality infrastructure was created which enabled the city to offer its guests a warm welcome. Although this metamorphosis meant that ways of life, cultural values and memories of the past were lost or set aside, it only had a tolerable impact on the natural environment, including the unusual vertically structured, sunny architecture. These qualities were what made it the place of choice, even in the post-war period, for many world-famous artists and intellectuals: playwrights Aldo De Benedetti, Giulio Cesare Viola, Sergio Pugliese, Umberto Onorato and Eduardo de Filippo; actors Antonio de Curtis, better known as Totò, Andreina Pagnani, Alberto Sordi, Isabella Quarantotti De Filippo, Giorgio De Lullo; motion-pictures directors Vittorio De Sica and Franco Zeffirelli; Maestro Roman Vlad; dancer Rudolf Nureyev; set-designer Raimonda Gaetani and writer Niccolò Ammanniti, who won the prestigious Viareggio literary prize in 2001.

Previous page:
Balcony, by Michele Theile

Opposite:
Bridge at Positano, by Anita Rée

Below:
Fishing boat being pulled ashore, by Antonello Marinucci
(collection of Positano Town Council)

Raffaele Bella – initiated, as a favourite pupil, by Vincenzo Caprile into the secrets of painting while Caprile was in Positano - is the leading Positano artist who gained international recognition and success. He had a complex and versatile artistic personality and was obviously influenced by the Neapolitan School. He loved painting, sculpture, playing the violin, writing poetry and stories for children. Bella was also a refined sculptor, the only one in Positano, and he loved sculpting small animals. He became world-famous after he did a sculpture of a gazelle for the Chamber of Commerce in Salerno.

He was loved and admired by all the artists, foreigners and Italians alike, who sought refuge in Positano and wanted to be as free as birds. He loved living in the Fornillo area in the house which many claimed belonged to Flavio Gioia and which he shared with his wife Rajzla Szlumiel, a Polish Jew who came to Positano as a refugee, and their two children Stenio and Elio. A third child, Elio's twin, died in tender age. Although he was an artist of international renown, he never went after success or glory and shied away from honour and awards. He preferred to live modestly and quietly in his retreat in Positano where he loved to work and play the violin after the sun had gone down. He died at age 67 on 23 July 1969. Along these same lines, there are quite a few more names that claim to be mentioned, such as:

Gioacchino Parlato, a winner at the first sailing Olympics in 1960.

Previous page:
Positano, by Giuseppe Di Lieto, 1926-2003 (collection of Casa Albertina Hotel)

Opposite:
Concetta Fiorentino, by Ettore Pignone del Carretto.

Below:
The Siren Partenope, by Laura Libera Lupo

Michele Theile, the most famous and loved painter in Positano, who studied with Karli Sohn-Rethel and Kurt Krämer during the war.

Nazario Fusco who, though he moved to Sardinia, never lost touch with his birthplace and still continues to paint its stone steps and more picturesque corners.

Aniello Cinque, who graduated in theatre-set design from the Fine Arts Academy in Naples, and remained very attached to his birthplace, its culture and his beloved Nocella, as can be seen from his work.

Ettore Pignone del Carretto, Gioacchino Parlato, the painter and set designer Roberto Scielzo, who did the set design and costumes for the extras in *Lo sbarco dei Saraceni*, Laura and Ugo Passalacqua who, although not actually born in Positano, adopted it as their home, along with Giuseppe Di Lieto and Ed Wittstein, Rob-

ert Miller, Peter Ruta, Jeanne Kotzé Louw – one of whose mosaics can be seen at the Fondazione Culturale Orfeo – Harriet Lovitt Damm, Maria Tourou, Liz Reday, Armanda Eller, Kirby Susan Malloy and many others who trained at the Art workshop, the school that the American artist Edna Lewis set up in the Sixties.

We should also remember the painter Vali Myers, who died not long ago, and the artists Rudolf Rappold and Gianni Menichetti (winner of the prize "Amico Rom" di Lanciano with his work *Poems to the Gypsies*) who together fought hard to preserve the Vallone Porto oasis. And also the Albanian painter Ibrahim Shaban Likmetaj Kodra, Athos Faccincani, Katinka Niederstrasser, Eduardo De Gregori, Ottavio Romano, Paolo Santulli, Domenico Marrone, Laura Libera Lupo and so many others, from Positano and outside.

F. peregrinus

A honourable mention goes to John Steinbeck who, with his article on Positano published in 1953 in the American magazine *Harper's Bazaar*, enabled Americans to discover the place. Also to Maestro Wilhelm Kempff who came to Positano on his honeymoon and returned in 1957 to set up the Fondazione Culturale Orfeo, a special school for talented young musicians. Positano awarded honorary citizenship to this world-famous musician in 1975[32].

In the post-war years, cinema also discovered Positano, and many Italian and foreign films were set there, including, amongst others, *Un marito per Anna Zaccheo* directed by Giuseppe De Santis, *La fiamma e la carne* with Silvana Pampanini, and *Leoni al sole*. A long series of scientific and ethnographical documentaries were also made here.

Guests from the world of show-business include Emma Gramatica, Liz Taylor and Richard Burton, who fell in love with Li Galli islands and did all he could to buy them, Ronald Reagan with his wife Nancy, Anita Ekberg and many more.

More recent visitors include Prince Rainier of Monaco and Grace Kelly, Jacqueline Kennedy, Princess Margaret, the Rolling Stones and the folk singer Shawn Phillips, who wrote here some of his most famous songs.

Fishing and farming traditions – the twin souls of Positano – stay alive, along with that innate sense of hospitality which has helped the town gain and maintain its honoured status as one of the world's leading tourist resorts. Positano also features on the international fashion map. There are a large number of cottage industries, countless workshops and smart shops selling brightly-coloured clothes that line the town's narrow streets. They cater to the tastes of a demanding international clientele and provide ample testimony to the independent and entrepreneurial spirit that has always distinguished the people of Positano.

NOTES

[1] One legend has it that S. Antonino and S. Catello, patron saints of Sorrento and Castellammare di Stabia respectively, retired to our hills to lead a more contemplative life. One day, they saw a dazzling golden light enveloping the archangel Michael that inspired them to build a place of worship dedicated to him. It is more likely, however, that San Michele chapel was built on the site of a previous temple to the god Mithra.

[2] It was given its current name after the local look-out and defence tower was built in 1566 on the orders of the Viceroy, Dom Pedro de Toledo, because it had a bell in its armoury which could be used to sound the alarm if an enemy fleet was sighted.

[3] Apart from this cave and the Mezzogiorno cave to the west of Positano, nobody has ever found out exactly how many caves there are in our area.

[4] Romolo Ercolino, *L'Isola delle Sirene - Li Galli*, Castellammare di Stabia, 1997.

[5] Homer, *Iliad*, XIV 324-5.

[6] S. Vito Martyr was also the protector of the town of Paestum before it was destroyed by the Saracens.

[7] The term "Saracen" was used by the Greeks to describe people from the East or from the desert. Saracens intended as "Sarah's descendants" is a mediaeval invention.

[8] Matteo Camera, *Memorie storico-diplomatiche dell'antica Città e Ducato di Amalfi*, vol. II, Salerno 1881, p. 686.

[9] Fernand Braudel, *Civiltà e Imperi del Mediterraneo nell'età di Filippo II*, Torino 1976.

[10] It would appear that the magnetic needle was already used in China, and in France under the name *marinette*. The Provençal troubadour, Guiot de Provins (b. circa 1145, d. after 1208) refers to it in one of his songs, which translates thus: "When the sea is dark and murky, when neither the sun nor the moon can be seen, they [the navigators] cast light at the needle and they don't worry about going off course as the point turns toward the star".

[11] The first reference to a watermill is in the epigram written by the general and poet Antipater (b. circa 390 BC) when he was fighting with Alexander the Great's Phalanx in the East, and saw them working: "Oh you young girls, working the mills, stop your toil; sleep and wait for the birds to sing at sunrise; the goddess of harvest has already ordered the nymphs to do your work, and the obedient nymphs threw themselves at the wheels: the axles vigorously turned round and, with them, the heavy grinding machines". In the *Antologia Palatina* (IX, 418) Antiphilus of Byzantium, an epigrammatist of Augustan age, wrote: "Sleep longer even if the cock crow sounds the new day: Demeter has charged the nymphs to do the work you usually do. They are rushing on to the wheels and making the axle turn, whose screw mechanism moves the concave weight of Nizyra's millstones. We will experience a new Golden Age if we learn to enjoy Demeter's work without pain".

[12] The Saracen galley was a light ship with fifteen or twenty oars on each bank and was faster than other ships because the hull, in order to reduce friction, was continually smeared with tallow to prevent shipworms sticking to it.

[13] "To all castle-masters: so that we know when you sight enemy vessels approaching, we ask you to use smoke signals by day and fire signals at night, and to indicate how many enemy galleons or military vessels there are by the number of signals you send".

[14] "Robert King of Naples (…) informed Pietro de Cadeneto and Giovanni Spinello di Giovinazzo, his counsellors on the Administration of the Vicarage of the Kingdom of the following: It has come to our notice that enemy pirates, who sail our seas in galleys and other boats, are attacking the Amalfi Coast too often, causing extensive damage to our subjects there. It has also come to our notice that the people from towns and villages [along the Coast] who have to navigate those waters, have suffered loss of lives, damage to their properties and general hardship. We, therefore, decree that in the area around Li Galli islands, a fort or a tower be built which will keep constant watch day and night over people who are faithful to us, including our subjects and other merchants who sail these waters. In this way, they will be protected from the dangers of robbery and attack at the hands of hostile pirates who haunt those waters. To make sure that our proposal be enacted, we would like to establish that a fairly tall tower be built according to plans presented to His Majesty by Mr. Pasquale Celentano, a subject

from Positano, on a piece of uncultivated land close to the Amalfi Coast on Li Galli islands, which seems the best place. Our Treasury will contribute 10 gold ounces to the project in advance, and Pasquale Celentano will put forward the other 13 ounces to complete the project. Once it is finished he will let the Treasury take out a mortgage on the building on condition that he can be master of the tower for life. Apart from Celentano, another four soldiers will be assigned to the tower. These will be recruited by the Royal Court and paid 8 tarens a month while Celentano will earn 10 as he requested. We would also like to establish that the 13 ounces Celentano is going to advance will be paid back by the following towns: Amalfi will pay back 3 ounces, Atrani 10 tarens, Minori 20 tarens, Maiori 1 ounce, Tramonti 1 ounce, Ravello 2 ounces, Scala 1 ounce and 1/5 of a taren, Agerola 1 ounce, Conca 15 tarens, Positano 1 ounce and Capri 1 ounce. The various towns are enjoined to respect these arrangements".

[15] Arienzo was the name of an old Positano family.

[16] 29 May 1453 was a Tuesday, and from then onwards Tuesday was considered an unlucky day.

[17] A Calabrian folk song gives an idea of the terror the Turkish incursions spread around: *All'armi! All'armi! La campana sona! Li Turchi sunne iunti alla marina…* (Take up your weapons! Take up your weapons! The bell sounds! The Turks have arrived at our shore!)

[18] When the Christian fleet made its victorious return to Messina, people celebrated with a song which translates this way: "Long live Messina and the Royal Eagle / the night is over and the sun will rise now / the cross reigns supreme on our seas / the Turks no longer venture there / those treacherous dogs are dead".

[19] Francesco Barra, *La Costa di Amalfi nell'età moderna. Economia e società*, in "La costa di Amalfi nel secolo XVII", published by the Amalfi Centre for Culture and History, Amalfi 2003, I, pp. 7-34.

[20] Giuseppe Maria Galanti, *Della descrizione geografica e politica delle Sicilie*, vol. III, Napoli 1794.

[21] Francesco Barra, *La Costa d'Amalfi…*, cit., p. 18.

[22] From General Montbrun's report to General Berthier, in *Cronache militari e marittime del golfo di Napoli e delle isole Pontine durante il decennio francese (1806-15), di Umberto Broccoli*, Roma 1953.

[23] G. M. Galanti, *Della descrizione…*, cit.

[24] O. Caterini in *Il Giorno* newspaper dated 1 June 1924.

[25] Clavel was an expert in the esoteric Tibetan doctrine, introduced by H. P. Blavatsky to Europe with his *La dottrina segreta*, which claimed 5 to be the perfect number.

[26] Eduard Ghillhausen was awarded honorary citizenship in 1986, sixty years after his arrival.

[27] The famous donkey with the panniers, which became the symbol of Vietri sul Mare and the Amalfi Coast, is by Dolker.

[28] On 20 October 2005, a hundred years after his birth, the town of Baku and the German-Azer Association headed by Cingiz Abdullayev, chose to honour their famous citizen - whose work was relatively unknown in his homeland because of political turmoil - by organising a large conference with experts and scholars from all over the world. The speakers included: Hasan Guliyev, Zeydulla Agayev, Elcin Musa Oglu, Tafik Malik Jabbosav, Nana Gaprindasvili and Jvana Giavakishvili from Georgia State University, the German film director Ralf Marschalleck and Romolo Ercolino.

[29] Comprehensive biographies on Essad Bey were written by his fellow countryman Hasan Guliyev in 2002, and by Tom Reiss with *L'orientalista, l'ebreo che volle essere un principe musulmano*, Milano 2006.

[30] The name derives from the watering trough for animals, as the Italian inscription above it reminds us: "This trough, donated by Lady Banbury, was built and is now maintained by the Italian League for the Protection of Animals".

[31] "…To General Sir William D. Morgan K.C., D.S.O., M.C. [King's Cross, Distinguished Service Order, Military Cross], in his capacity as Chief of Staff [of Field Marshal Sir Harold Alexander] during the [final] period of the Battle of Italy and later Supreme Commander of the Mediterranean Exchequer, who has proved himself a true friend and fervent admirer of Italy's beauty on many occasions.

Positano was at that time chosen as a Rest Camp for officers from His Majesty's armed forces and the town's people always enjoyed a good relationship with the English based on mutual friendship, understanding and respect. It was the Supreme Commander's kindness and generosity that fostered such relationship, so beneficial for Positano - a town small in terms of extension and number of inhabitants but large in terms of beauty and the emotion it inspires. General Sir William D. Morgan is thus known as a close and personal friend of Positano, which is why I [the Mayor] would like to express to him, in official terms, the gratitude and thanks the whole population feels for him. On account of the above, I hereby confer on General Sir William D. Morgan K.C.,D.S.O.,M.C., the title of Honorary Citizen of Positano".

(Parchment housed in the Positano City Hall)

[32] "…To Maestro Wilhelm Kempff, thanks to whose work the name and fame of Positano spread through Europe and the rest of the world. Maestro Kempff, one of the most famous orchestra conductors honoured throughout the world and one of the greatest and most faithful interpreters of Beethoven's music, has been coming to Positano for a number of years and created here, in 1957, the Fondazione Culturale Orfeo.

Standards at this school are extremely high and every year young musical talents from around the world gather here to follow higher courses in Beethoven's music and to compete for the Positano prize. Maestro Kempff chose Positano for his Cultural centre because of the profound spiritual bond that links him to our town and its people - the kind of bond most people share with their homeland and which prompts them to talk about it everywhere. When the famous conductor and his musicians travel around the world, they take with them not only their wonderful music but also memories of Positano's beauty. The people of Positano, appreciative and grateful for the honour accorded them by the Maestro and, at the same time, deeply fond of him, have asked on several occasions that he be awarded honorary citizenship. Mindful of these requests, the Council, after reading the President's report, has decided to award Maestro Wilhelm Kempff the honorary citizenship of Positano".
(Parchment housed in the Positano City Hall)

JOURNEYS
THROUGH
MEMORY

Most visitors, hasty tourists and pleasure-seekers see Positano as a place to relax and have fun. A more careful observer, however, can see the hidden soul beneath, discover the monuments which few people know about and wipe away the dust that has settled on the pages of history. Positano's isolation, and the difficulty in getting there, helped to preserve a heritage of unique architecture and landscape. Because the environment has not undergone any major changes, the place has preserved its charm and beauty.

The thick, flourishing woodland and the abundance of running water made it possible for craftsmen to set up workshops on an almost industrial level. There were shipyards, ovens for producing lime, looms and water mills.

To really trace what remains of the past, one needs to go into the bowels of the town, and follow the old footpaths which are much more interesting and exciting than the normal tourist itineraries. They offer amazing, unexpected views and allow seeing works that, over the centuries, shaped the human landscape and current layout of our town.

Only one road, the Strada Statale 163, has linked Positano to the rest of the world since the closing years of 19th century. This scenic road, full of hairpin bends as it follows the contour lines of the precipitous mountain (and to some degree of the coastline) through bare rock and under great overhangs, enabled wayfarers to admire the wild beauty of the landscape with its deep gorges and crowning green hills.

"At a certain point, the road crosses over the ridge of the peninsula and you suddenly see the sea of the bay of Salerno

on the other side. It opens out on the distant horizon where, on clearer days, you can make out Capo Palinuro in a kind of blue haze, and where you can see the small Sirenuse [Li Galli] islands near the coast. At this precise point, you feel almost dizzy, suspended in the air as if you were on a roller-coaster at the fair.

The road clings tightly to the mountain-side and all around you can see vertical drops, narrow gullies and gorges which are wild and scary and without a house or a tree. Ahead lies a series of breathtaking bends overlooking the sea, which shimmers in all its blueness so far below. The tarmac road winds its way through rocky barriers from one abyss to another and at every turn you get the feeling you might be sucked into the surrounding nightmare.

The first time I took the road I was so amazed, charmed yet completely overcome, that I felt almost dizzy and wasn't sure whether it was the emotion, or car-sickness after driving round so many bends, to make me feel that way. I asked the driver to stop so I could recover.

What I saw was a raw, unusual beauty, unthinkable for anyone coming from the gentle Sorrento. There was nothing pleasurable about the landscape, no feeling could describe it. Its beauty was absolute and grandiose, rebellious, out of man's reach.

This was my first impression of the Amalfi Coast, and it seemed like a different world to me that day, with its incredibly dramatic and intense character, light and colours. But after lots more bends and steep mountains dropping away to the

sea below, I finally saw the white houses of Positano crowded like baby goats on a verdant slope. And when I saw the beach with the church in the middle, and those glinting yellow and blue tiles on its cupola, it all looked so welcoming and so pleasant on that bright morning so long ago, that it felt like coming back to somewhere I had been before and where I immediately felt to belong[1]".

Coming from Sorrento, after about twelve kilometres of narrow twisting road, where every bend offers a different view, it is almost compulsory to stop at the Belvedere – once the station for the collectors of duties on goods entering the town – marked by a marble statue of the Madonna.

From its terraces, which overlook the sea as from prows cutting through the waves, one gets a great and unexpected view which takes in the emerald-blue sea and the green hilltops crowning the town. It is possible to admire the pentagonal Torre di Fornillo, renovated at the beginning of the 20th century by Clavel, Li Galli (or Sirenuse) islands and appreciate the architectural harmony of the old, square, variously coloured houses lining the shore. With their traditional vaulted roofs, these houses are specimens of Mediterranean architecture, whose features have remained unchanged over the centuries. Built on the slopes, they follow the natural lie of the land: the resulting gardens and residential areas are uneven and ill defined but all of them are exposed to the sun. The imposing Monte S. Angelo a Tre Pizzi (m. 1443) looms over

Previous page:
The Chiesa Nuova district

Below:
Liparlati

the place. On its austere but fascinating slopes lie the ancient mountain villages of Montepertuso and Nocella and, further down, Laurito.

The first urban district of Positano proper is Chiesa Nuova with its monumental church, which dominates the entire town and gave its name on one of the earliest settlements.

If coming from Amalfi or by sea, once past the Capo Sottile in Praiano, you will be amazed at the pyramid of multicoloured houses rising up from the main beach to Chiesa Nuova. This church forms an ideal tip to the pyramid, with just a few untoward recent architectural additions, trapped between the rocks and gardens.

When did Positano come into being? Since no documents have been found, it is impossible to assign precise birthdates to settlements such as Chiesa Nuova, Liparlati, Fornillo, Marina, Mulini, Sponda, Laurito, Montepertuso and Nocella. Until the Amalfi - Meta di Sorrento road, and the Pasitea and Cristoforo Colombo streets were built, and then the road up

to Montepertuso and Nocella, the only way to travel between these places was along difficult winding paths and steep steps, whose advantage was that they also provided a form of additional passive defence, as they discouraged even the most daring Saracens and Turks from venturing up there. These various settlements, originally isolated and perched on the hillsides, gradually grew and merged to form the beginnings of Positano.

A historical analysis of what is termed spontaneous architecture confirms this scheme of development. The style is homogeneous not only because of climate and environmental factors but also because of Mediterranean culture. The picture we get is of tiny settlements gradually growing in size until the advent of tourism and new construction techniques, which led to specifically designed buildings for the tourist industry and larger, more comfortable private housing. By following these old footpaths we can retrace the steps of our ancestors and find out more about them.

The Pathway of the Gods

From the Neolithic period onwards (15,000-10,000 years ago), as is proved by the archaeological finds in the La Porta cave, a complex network of footpaths crossed the Monti Lattari (which were eventually known as the *Sirenei Montes* or *Taurobulae* or *Lactarii Montes*[2]). As the population grew, so did the number of footpaths.

The most famous of these is the "Sentiero degli Dei", or Pathway of the Gods, which provided for millennia the only link between the two sides of the Sorrento Peninsula, and is still in use today. It was originally a branch of the old road from *Nuceria* through *Stabiae* to *Surrentum* and the Minerva temple. This stood at the end of the promontory known today as Punta Campanella but which at the time was called *Promontorium Minervae*. When it got to *Aequa*, known as Vico Equense today, there was a turn-off leading up to the higher villages and the other side of the Monti Lattari. The road was flanked by sanctuaries, like a small temple dedicated to the goddess of harvest, on the site of today's church of S. Maria del Castello. There was also a temple to the god Mithra which was superseded by S. Michele with the advent of Christianity. These sanctuaries provided resting places for pilgrims,

wanderers and shepherds, and many can still be found along the footpaths that today lead through the untamed, incomparable beauty of the Monti Lattari.

There are two footpaths up to S. Maria del Castello from Chiesa Nuova.

The first one starts close to the road junction up to Montepertuso and follows the valley of river Noce up as far as Capo d'Acqua or Headwater – although the river has practically dried up now. It then ascends on to the S. Maria del Castello plain (about 700 m. above sea level). At the beginning of this path a couple of disused lime furnaces can be noticed. Higher up, on a ledge, there is a period farmhouse in a truncated-pyramid shape, which dominates the valley and is reminiscent of a fort. The Jewish writer, Armin Teophil Wegner, who was one of many political refugees to come here during the WW2 years, lived in this house. The higher you climb, the wilder the surrounding countryside becomes, and steeper and more difficult the path. After over an hour's rewarding – if wearysome – walk one finally gets to S. Maria del Castello.

The other path starts off at Via Corvo, in the higher part of Chiesa Nuova. It runs through the open, easy Tese di S. Giuseppe, a stairway built in 1827 at the cost of nine hundred ducats, and attains, after about an hour's walk, the S. Maria del Castello plain. Along the path, high on the escarpment, is the entrance to a cave. Ensconced in the surrounding rock and partly walled over, it has inside a slit for firearms. It is said that this almost inaccessible cave was

101

Previous page:
Approaching Positano from the "Pathway of the Gods"

Opposite:
A signpost at Nocella

Below:
One of the small cascades along Vallone Porto

used as a robber hideout, and as an escape route in an emergency, having another exit in the Noce river valley. The cave does not, in fact, go much further inside than it appears from the path, and perhaps it was used by some hermits in the late Middle Ages and as a checkpoint in more recent times, when the path provided the only link between the two sides of the peninsula. Halfway along the path is a shrine to S. Giuseppe. Along the tese there are steps carved into the rock as well as *pose*, that is rough, rock-hewn seats siding the way for passers-by to rest.

From the lofty, pleasant village of S. Maria del Castello one of the best views in the world can be savoured: the whole of Positano, the blue sea, Li Galli islands, the Gulf of Salerno and the Gulf of Naples.

The little church is worth a visit with its precious works of art including a 17th-century marble statue of the Madonna and some Neapolitan paintings of the same epoch. The path takes through Castagnole – the chestnut village – a small farming community, practically deserted now, where the view of the bay of Salerno is stunning. The mountain scenery is supremely beautiful with breathtaking views and colours. The natural environment is also very interesting with its dense beech, ash, fir, cypress, live oak and chestnut woodland as well as what remains of the original Mediterranean maquis: rosemary, mastic, broom, juniper and myrtle.

On the way, the song of blackcaps and great titmouses can be heard and, with a bit of luck, a kestrel, peregrine falcon, buzzard or other rare visiting bird can be sighted.

Occasionally, one can stumble upon fox footprints, or even traces of wild boar, recently returned to our mountains. The presence here of a *calcàra*, the typical limestone furnace, shows how important lime was in the past. In one of the many caves along the way there is a statue of the Madonna of S. Maria del Castello and an engraved stone memorial.

A bit further up from Castagnole lies an old forestry barracks, built during the 1920s for the reforestation work and now used as a mountain refuge. This is where a track, branching to the east from of the Pathway of the Gods, leads to Cava de' Tirreni through the Lattari mountainsides and valleys mantled with dense woodland and chiselled with narrow cultivated terraces.

More sets of the old *pose* occur along these paths. As previously hinted to, these were resting or meeting places for people who took to the mountains out of necessity rather than pleasure, usually to look for firewood and forage for their animals, or to transport produce on back-sacks from one side of the mountain to the other.

Lots of other tracks intersect or diverge from the main path, so there are plenty of alternative routes up to Montepertuso and Nocella, where something to eat and drink can be had, before continuing up to Monte S. Angelo a Tre Pizzi, Agerola, or just wandering around to discover the beauties of the Monti Lattari.

Previous page:
Mimosa in bloom

Opposite:
Li Galli, a stretch of the seacoast

Below:
Li Galli from Via S. Croce

Li Galli Isles

"...*while on the other side of the Cape* [Punta della Campanella], *looking towards the Gulf of Posidonia* [the Gulf of Paestum, now the Gulf of Salerno], *there are three unhinabited rocky little islands called the Sirenuse[3]*".

There are some historical events of which no record exists, only a faded image. As time goes by, myth and legend tend to blend with the facts, especially where far-away places are concerned. Sailors would talk about the wonders they had seen and embellish reality with their imagination.

This was the case with Li Galli or Sirenuse islands, the tiny archipelago lying about three miles off Positano, formed by Il Gallo Lungo, La Rotonda and I Briganti (or San Pietro) islands. They have guarded their pages

of history so jealously that many are still unread. In ancient times, they were believed to be the home of Homer's mythical two sirens (whom he doesn't name), Telxiope ("of the mesmerizing beauty") and Aglaope ("of the wonderful voice") who were so distraught that they had failed to capture Ulysses (because Circe had told him what to do to escape their charms) that they hurled themselves into the sea[4]. From then on, the Sirens became three, Parthenope ("the virginal"), Leucosia ("the resplendent") and Ligia or Ligeia ("of the resounding voice). Their sweet song and fascinating looks lured to shipwrecks the sailors, whom they then dismembered[5].

The Phoenicians, the first people to colonize the Western Mediterranean, were the first to claim possession of the islands, followed by the Greeks and then the Romans. Once the Romans had deported the Piceni

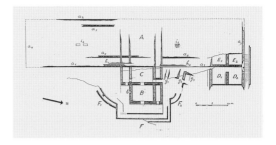

rebels to the Salerno area, they established the Sirenuse as the border to their new territory. In the 1st century AD, a patrician, maybe one of Emperor Tiberius courtiers, built a villa there, which became a monastery after the fall of the Empire. A Saracen invasion led by Boalìm in 991 was described as follows: *"…They headed for the nearby Li Galli islands and landed on the largest, where there was a monastery. They sent the swift and agile Ethiopians, who were with them, to actually get in. This enabled them to climb in, using ropes thrown over the monastery walls. Once inside they found the monk, Arsenio, three other monks and a layman. They killed Arsenio and took the others prisoner. As they left, they took everything they could from the S. Bartolomeo altar and then destroyed it[6]"*.

During the period of the Amalfi Dukedom the Sirenuse were used as a prison stronghold. Giovanni II, the doge, ordered his brother Mansone IV, who had attempted to depose him, to be blinded and deported there.

In 1225, Emperor Federico II issued a special decree handing over Li Galli islands and fishing rights in their waters to the abbey of Positano.

In 1332 Robert of Anjou ordered that a fort and a watchtower be built there. This was because the islands had become a hideout for Saracen pirates who ambushed the ships navigating the area, and organized raids on local towns, taking people prisoner and then selling them as slaves. Pasquale Celentano of Positano who offered to build the tower and finance it himself, was given in return the post of castellano (castle master) for life. This was

the first in a set of towers built along the coast during the Angevin period. Celentano built fortifications on the Rotonda and Briganti islands as well. For centuries considered part of frontline military defence because of their position, after the unification of Italy the islands were no longer of any use and were sold to private owners. During the 1920s, the famous Russian dancer and choreographer Léonide Massine bought them to create a haven for himself and his family. In the 1980s, they went to another famous Russian ballet dancer, Rudolf Nurejev. Li Galli now belong to a consortium of tourism operators from Sorrento.

Of the Roman villa built on Gallo Lungo only one of the two landings and the cistern remain. On the Briganti island the slipway carved into the rock to pull the boats up is still visible and, further up, the ruins of a rather inaccessible mediaeval fort. Li Galli not only represent one of the richest sources of history on the whole Amalfi coast, but its crags are also famous as the realm of blue lizards, a rare species which also survives on the nearby Vivara islet – being almost extinct on the Faraglioni di Capri and Punta della Campanella. The subspecies *Lacerta sicula gallensis* and the *Lacerta sicula massinei*[7] are endemic to these islands.

The Roman Villas

Over the first few centuries of the Roman Empire, many patricians built luxury houses along the Campania coast for themselves. The oldest architectural remains in our own territory are the Roman villas of Li Galli and Positano.

The first one, built on the Gallo Lungo in the 1st century AD, has practically disappeared. Before Léonide Massine bought the island in the 1920s and started work on the current residence, archaeologists P. Mingazzini and F. Pfister found remains of the *domus*, the ample terrace-garden (*xystus*) and the two constructions on the beach with their respective landings. Today's villa, built by Massine, stands on the foundations of the Roman villa – so it has covered all traces of the same. Only the water cisterns and the steps leading up to the villa and garden can still be seen.

The historic 79 AD eruption of Vesuvius that destroyed Herculaneum, Pompeii and Stabiae, which is known as the archetype of "Plinian" eruptions, also covered the Monti Lattari in a layer of ash and lapilli[9]. A few days later, a massive rainstorm carried huge flows of mud and debris down the hillsides. The Positano villa, which was built behind the main beach near the estuary of the Valle Pozzo river, was completely buried under a landslide some 20m in thickness.

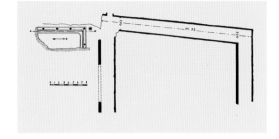

This villa dates back to the beginning of the 1st century AD but it is not known who built it nor how big it was. This is because the excavation work, carried out to rob it of archaeological artefacts and to quarry the sand and lapilli, used at that time for the external waterproofing on the traditional vaulted roofs of the older Positano houses, erased any evidence that might have helped identify who built the villa and when.

The first official report on the house was written in 1758 by the Swiss architect Karl Weber, director of excavation works at the ancient Villa dei Papiri in Herculaneum. After reading a dispatch written by a man from Positano by the name of Giovanni Atanasio (the owner of the area), the Bourbon King Charles sent Weber to Positano to inspect the site and the archaeological finds[10].

Weber ordered the immediate stop to the excavations because he worried for the stability of the Chiesa dell'Assunta campanile. All memory of the villa was thus removed until 1921 when Vincenzo Imperato, an old butcher, discovered the entrance to the villa while deepening a cave near his shop to keep meat fresh (Positano had no electricity at the time, so the cool of natural caves was used untill the advent of refrigerators). In 1931, thanks to the Mingazzini and Pfister, an in-depth study was carried out and the following report produced:

"[The excavated part] *looks like the NW corner of a peristile, with plaster-covered, fluted brick columns surrounding a garden (viridarium), and an adjoining very large rectangular enclosure (xystus), probably planted with fruit trees bordered by shaded,*

Previous page:
Via Trara Genoino: *la scalinatella* or Little Stairway

Below:
La scalinatella in a vintage photograph

Page 120:
The fisher woman, by Amerigo Tot, 1956 (a gift from Tobia Salino to Positano Town Council)

Page 122:
Via San Giovanni

Page 123:
Head detail of the cast iron lion seen on page 42

windowed walkways, once protected by a roof-covering (ambulatio-solarium). Very little remains of the mural stucco decoration. As to the material burying the ruins, there is no doubt at all that it is the well-known fallout products of the 79 AD Plinian eruption".

A fresco fragment was thus described by another archaeologist: *"At the bottom is the blue sea. In the middle, columns and doors. On the top, the legs of a mythical beast".*

Not long after, under the direction of the Naples Superintendence of Excavations, the few ruins that had been brought to light were surveyed and sketched.

More recently, the Salerno Archaeological Superintendence has directed the uncovering of other details, frescoes and objects from the villa.

Are these descriptions and the partial survey the only historical clues as to the past of this buried Roman villa?

Under Via Trara Genoino (immortalised in the song by Bonagura and Cioffi entitled Scalinatella, one of the late singer Roberto Murolo showpieces) lie the remains of three arch-vaulted rooms and, perpendicular to them, an arch shoulder belonging to a ruined building. After careful study and comparison with the construction techniques used for the cisterns of other Roman villas, especially those on Li Galli and Punta Campanella, it can reasonably be assumed that the arch was part of the cistern or the aqueduct belonging to the ancient Roman villa.

[1] Raffaele La Capria, *Ultimi viaggi nell'Italia perduta*, Napoli 1992.

[2] The name *Sirenei Montes* clearly refers to the myth of the Sirens; *Taurobulae* to the good quality beef from cows reared on our mountains; *Lactarii* to the excellence of milk and dairy products thanks to the unusual aromatic grasses which the cows, sheep and goats grazed in the pastures of this mountain range.

[3] Strabo, *Geography*, I, 2, 12.

[4] Homer's *Odyssey*, Book XII, 230-43: "*I stopped with wax the ears of my shipmates, one by one. On the ship, they bound me right away to the mast with ropes, tightening my hands and feet. Then they sat at the rovers' benches and went racing and churning with their oars the seawater to a white foam. Scudding with fury, we were just a man's shout close to the Sirens. As these sensed the oars' rhythmic pulse and saw the ship approaching, they started to voice a sweet song: «Oh most illustrious Odysseus, oh you of the Achaeans' highest immortal glory, come on, rest your ship and hear our song»*".

[5] Homer's *Odyssey*, Book XII, 45-6: "*...but the sweet song of the Sirens, lolling in their meadows, will transfix him; round them heaps of human corpses rotting away, rags of skin shrivelling on their bones*".
See also Virgil's Aeneid, Book V, 1231-5: "*Already the ship, pushed by the wind, was approaching the siren's reefs, once infamous and white with a multitude of* [human] *bones*".

[6] From the paper by Antonio Mattiello, *Boalim, pirata saraceno*, e Capri published in "Capri e l'Islam", Capri 2002.

[7] The name *Lacerta sicula massinei* given to this type of lizard was coined in honour of the famous choreographer by R. Mertens because Massine not only invited him to stay in his house on the Gallo Lungo island while he was conducting his research, but was also very helpful when it came to catching the lizards on the nearby Rotonda.

[8] "*The villa stood on the largest of the three islands making up the small archipelago called Li Galli. It is a miniature version of the seaside villas found at Capo di Sorrento and on the Massa* [Lubrense] *point. The domus is built on the summit of the island with a large adjoining terrace, which is set out as a garden or xystus. There are buildings down by the sea each with their own landing ... We know how big it was: 15.25 m. x 66.50 m.*". From *Forma Italiae, Surrentum*, Firenze 1946, p. 147.

[9] Ash and lapilli can still be seen in hollows in the Valle Pozzo and in other parts of the area.

[10] "*Portici 23 April 1758. This is in answer to a request expressed by Your Excellency when I handed over the dispatch by Giovanni Atanasio, native of the royal land of Positano. On the 16th I crossed the mountains and came to the aforementioned place and immediately prepared the dig to be able to check whether the monument, so precisely described in the dispatch, was the same one. Digging continued until the 20th. During that time I was able to see that to the side of the church with the bell-tower that faces the beach, to the south-east at the foot of the S. Maria del Castello and S. Angelo mountains of the Costa di Amalfi, at a depth of about 36 palms* [one palm equals about 25 cm], *there lies a famous old building. The first mosaic we found is in white marble and of a beautiful quality, but we haven't found any engraving yet. The lapilli had obviously been removed to be employed as construction material near the campanile, and the way things develop appear to indicate that the ancient temple lies underneath the church. The presbyter and sacristan don Giuseppe Vianiero told me that they had dug down and found various archaeological remains, such as columns, and used them for the church. This would seem to be true given the various mosaics and old green and yellow marble slabs I saw on the floor in the presbytery. He also said they sold columns and other archaeological remains to the S. Teresa delle Monache monastery in Naples, and it was thanks to their generosity and money that it was possible to make the church much bigger than it was before. According to him, all of this happened at the end of the last century, but it would have to be checked with the Regia Camera as the church no longer has any archival material because it was destroyed in a Saracen raid. After the aforementioned mosaic, moving away from the church, there are some small rooms with painted walls showing ornaments, vases, griffins, goats, leaves etc. but much of the coloured plaster work has collapsed because it was in such bad condition. Atanasio however kept a*

few fragments. I then saw two large brick columns, coloured bright red, standing at each side of a large round stone fountain, the delight of the garden. Past it there is another entrance similar to the first one, with whitewashed brick columns and, to the side, a rectangular-shaped garden whose longer side measures about 200 palms, surrounded by a corridor with tiled floor and whitewashed columns, with a large basin in the middle complete with drainage pipe. This is what I was able to see before issuing orders to Atanasio to close and seal the first cave with stones and compacted earth, along with three stone pillars to protect the campanile. It would be a good idea to send two excavation experts from the Royal Site [Herculaneum] who can work with the four other men from here so that they can finish the job within fifteen days. Weber".

[11] From *Forma Italiae, Surrentum*, cit., p. 356-9.

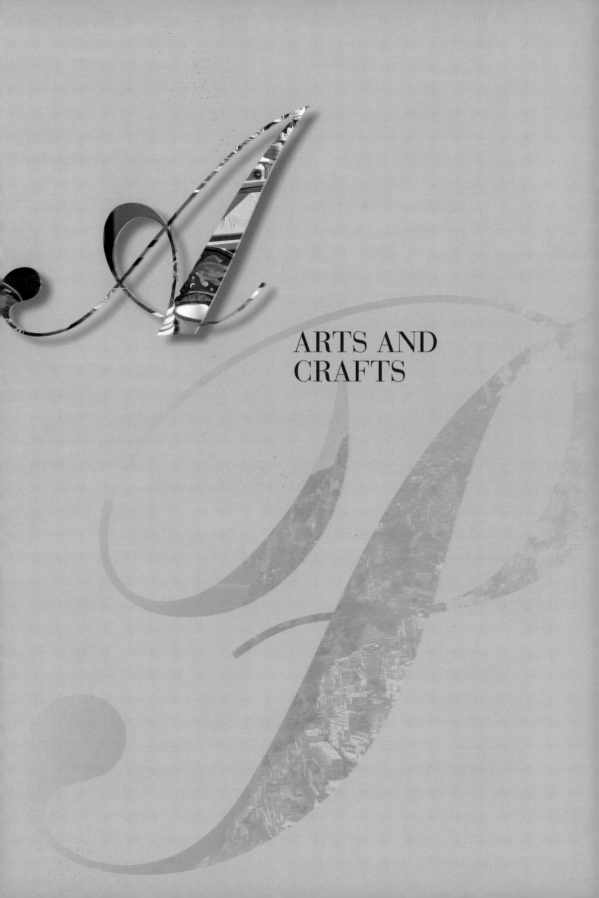

ARTS AND CRAFTS

The mills

Place names unchanged over the years enable us to trace the historic links between craftsmen and the mills in this area. "Valle dei Mulini" and "Piazza dei Mulini" remind us that the grinding of cereals and pulses using the water power harnessed from the Valle Pozzo river, through an ingenious system of mills, was the predominant business in the area.

Water mills came to the West and Italy in the 1st century BC: the earliest mention of a water-mill was in an epigram by the poet-soldier Antipater[1], who, when fighting with Philip II of Macedonia and his son Alexander the Great, had admired the water mills in the Orient.

The Romans knew about this kind of mill but did not really use them. Vitruvius, in his book *De Architectura*, described how to build a mill using water rather than human power, even though slaves provided a huge source of cheap labour.

Water mills started to become popular in Europe around the year 1000 when this form of energy became the first step in a process that, centuries later, would make history as the "Industrial Revolution".

Mills became popular around Positano thanks to commercial and cultural links with the Arab world and especially with Sicily at the time when the island was under Arab domination. It was the Arabs who introduced this type of mill, which was

termed "Arab" and they remain unchanged today – as does the way that paper is made. The 10th-century Arab geographer Ibn Hauqal, in his work *kitab surat al-ardh* (Book illustrating the Earth), describes the mills around the city of Palermo where a stream turned several mills one after the other.

For many centuries the mills were the preserve of the rich, especially the clergy and monasteries, who had extensive sources of income and had royal privileges allowing them to take water from the rivers.

There were two types in use: vertical wheel mills if the water source was plentiful, and horizontal wheel mills, which needed less water and were thus more suitable to the kind of water flow in our area.

How many mills there were in Positano? Seven, according to Talamo, were active at the end of 19th century. Five of these were spaced out along the Valle Pozzo near the Valle dei Mulini and two, superimposed, were in Arienzo near the beach and the mouth of the Porto river. Nobody knows when they were built or by whom, nor, in-

deed, how many there were to start with. Sometimes the gaps left by history have to be plugged with documents and information, which, even if they do nor refer specifically to a particular issue, can shed some kind of light on it.

The Amalfi historian Matteo Camera, in his work *Memorie storico-diplomatiche dell'antica città e ducato di Amalfi*, when listing the various properties owned by the Benedictine abbey of S. Maria and S. Vito, included landed estates in Trapani which sent up the equivalent of 375 quintals of wheat, needed to feed the people connected to the abbey. We may argue from this that the first mills were built and run by the Benedictine monks, perhaps around the year 1000.

The five mills in the centre of Positano that Talamo talks about must have been built and variously renovated on the same site, as the land's morphology excludes anything else. Since it was impossible to build one large mill, the problem was solved by building a series of smaller mills and using every opportunity provided by the local water resources, unlike other kind of factories that had to be built, sometimes at quite a distance from towns, to get the water they needed.

In Positano, the presence of a river near the abbey and the beach made it easier, both for local people and for those bringing in their wheat by sea, to get it milled.

The unfavourable geography of our town was used to maximum effect by the mills. They followed the natural slopes and were placed so as to harness as much water power as possible. An artificial canal, called the main collector, gathered the water from the Valle Pozzo river in the Cascata district and channelled it into a large stone reservoir.

This served two purposes: to retain any rubble or foreign bodies that might otherwise damage the mill, and to ensure that the water supply could be adjusted to requirements. But the smartest idea, which we should credit to an unknown planner of ours, was to build a series of mills, which knowingly or unknowingly, resulted in accordance to Ibn Hauqal's description.

In this way, the water used by the first mill, once its work was done, fed the second mill and then turned the wheels of all the others downhill before being returned to the same riverbed it had come from higher up the mountain. It also meant that more than one mill could be used at contemporaneously.

In Giulio Rispoli's book, *Positano ieri e oggi*, there is a lovely photograph of the Valley of the Mills, taken in the 1930s. The five mills appear as they were before post-war building spree changed the place. Only the reservoir, part of the collector, the pressure tower and, a bit further up, along the feeder channel, a tank which served as a filter and to reduce the water pressure when necessary, have survived intact. The last mill, near the valley bottom, was demolished a few years ago to expand the sewage treatment works.

During the last war, as some people remember, the first of these mills was still in use and, in those times of great hardship, it ground not only cereals but also chestnuts that people picked in the woods of

S. Maria del Castello[2]. Post-war technological progress, changing work patterns and a tendency to abandon farming, signalled the end of this cottage industry.

Behind the beach in Arienzo still rises the old mill's pressure tower. It was built at the beginning of the 20th century, and later converted into a villa, though without changing its structure, by the Russian writer Michail Semenoff.

Its proximity to the beach confirms that it was accessible to people from neighbouring towns as well. They would come by sea as this was the only communication route between the various coastal towns.

The water for the mill came from the river Valle Porto. Along the right side of the valley, below the supporting wall for the new road, stand the remains of the collecting pipe and, further up, beyond the old road bridge, the reservoir. Once the mill closed, the reservoir was used as a tank to douse with water the product of nearby furnaces to turn it into quick-lime.

Talamo states that the Arienzo structure comprised two mills in close proximity. This is not supported by any document or witness account. The pressure tower was not high enough to turn two mills at the same time even if the wheels were horizontal. Carlo Knight's book "*La torre di Clavel*" (Capri 1999) confirms this point because he describes the old Arienzo mill as being furnished with a single millstone.

The olive presses

From the late Middle Ages onwards, olives, which had been introduced by the Basilian monks, were grown all over the area, and olive production and sales provided the main source of income for local farmers.

There were olive presses everywhere and the quality as well as the quantity of oil produced was impressive, ranging from 650 to 1.000 quintals per year. A large part of the oil was for local consumption and the surplus was sold to Naples and other towns. Over the last few years, as more and more people have left the countryside, olive trees tending has practically faded away and oil production has declined as a result.

Grapevines, also part of Mediterranean life for thousands of years, are slowly suffering the same fate.

Previous page:
Boutiques in Piazzetta del Saracino
Opposite and below:
Old looms

Canvas and silk

One of the many stone stairways criss-crossing the town of Positano is Via del Canovaccio which leads from Fornillo to Chiesa Nuova. This is another place-name which reminds us of one of the most important industries in the area, that is canvas making. It lasted for centuries and only died out towards the end of the Second World War. The reason this industry thrived, despite the fact that the raw materials had to be imported from far away, was because of the significant shipping industry based in Positano which, from the Middle Ages onwards, was second only to Amalfi. The ships needed large quantities of sturdy canvas and sailcloth, hence the decision to produce such ma-terials locally, and the reason for success of the enterprise. With the closure of the shipyards, and other historical events involving Positano, the canvas industry had to look for outlets elsewhere, and the local operators worked hard to adapt to changing demands within the market. However, the advent of artificial fabrics and large-scale industrial production, with its incomparable cost-effectiveness, sounded the death-knell for canvas production in Positano.

The canvas business, a source of such pride and notoriety for Positano, was first introduced by the Montuori family, among the oldest in Positano. It employed most of the women in town, as does the fashion industry today. The invisible thread of history always links past and present.

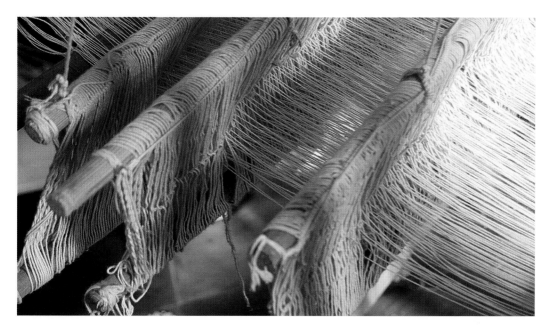

The rough hemp came from Terra di Lavoro, roughly today's Province of Caserta, where huge fields of *Cannabis sativa* could still be seen until a few decades ago. The textile fibre came from this herb, once its stems had been soaked in water to the point of rotting, and then dried and shaken free of the softer plant tissue.

The main trade and distribution centre for the product was Frattamaggiore near Naples. Traders from Positano bought the raw material there and transported it by carriage to Castellamare di Stabia and from there to Positano by sea.

The canvas material was worked in different ways depending on the end product wanted. Thick rough fibres were used to make rough cloths; thinner and softer ones – followed by a bleaching process which employed lime milk – if they needed to make bridal trousseaus of underwear, bed-sheets and linen. Any surplus product was exported to Naples, Salerno, Calabria and Sicily, places where many business people from Positano had settled. Talamo estimated that 1500 quintals of hemp were transformed yearly into canvas sheets or fabric in the Positano textile factories.

Our grandmothers also used to employ these natural fabrics as a panacea for headaches and to bring young babies' fevers down. There was even a well-developed recycling business running alongside. Threadbare canvases and untwisted ropes were made into sacks to transport coal and agricultural produce.

Again in Giulio Rispoli's book we can see a series of photographs showing the last people involved in this business before their remarkable vision and entrepreneurial spirit led them to abandon this now unprofitable activity and make themselves known to the world with their new product, Positano Fashion. This business has brought widespread fame to our town, but its historical roots lie in the production of canvas.

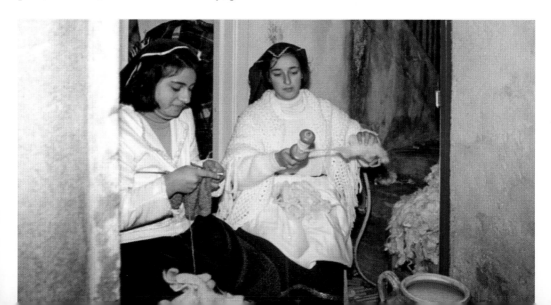

White mulberries (*Morus alba*), whose leaves were used to feed silkworms, were imported by the Arabs into Sicily and from there to the rest of Italy. Positano produced a thousand pounds of silk per year and most of the woven silk was embroidered and then exported. These were Positano's most expensive export product and, along with other luxury fabrics, they were sold in the markets in Naples, Salerno and other Italian and Mediterranean cities, where their beauty and finery were much appreciated. At the end of the 18th century, the plague that hit all the silkworm farms in Southern Italy signalled the end of this business.

Previous page:
Typical linen handicrafts

Opposite:
Tombolo lacework

Below:
Tombolo lace workshop in the 1950s

Hand-made lace

Hand-made *tombolo* (a drum-like supporting implement) lacework brought fame to our town thanks to the work of the Suore di Carità who, in their convent at the Chiesa Nuova, had, towards the end of the 19th century, set up a school to teach this noble art to the young ladies of Positano and the surrounding area. The art died out at the beginning of the 1960s.

Today only a few families have preserved a *tombolo* and its bobbins, and still fewer old ladies work at it.

Previous page:
Remains of a lime furnace in Nocella

Opposite:
Remains of a lime furnace in Castagnole

Below:
Remains of a lime furnace along the "Pathway of the Gods"

The calcàre *or lime furnaces*

"*...indomitusque silex curva fornace liquescit*" ...and the domed furnace undoes the indomitable stone. (P. P. Stazio, *Le selve*). Age-old lime production, one of the main cottage industries in Positano and on the Amalfi coast, went on till the 1950s – albeit with a slow, marked decline.

Over 30 furnaces (or *calcàre)* existed once in and around the area. Some are still fairly intact; others have almost disappeared.

At the end of 19th century, as stated by Talamo, 14 were still in use, 13 being wood-fired and just one, belonging to a certain Marcellino Montuori, coal-fired. The first furnaces were built along the coast, near the beach, to ease export of the end product. Smaller ones were built inland to satisfy local demand for construction, whitewashing (at the beginning of summer most of the houses in town were made to shine with a fresh hand of lime milk), farming, pest control and disinfection.

The last ones were built in the closing decades of the 19th century to meet the growing lime demand by companies engaged in the construction of the new road from Vietri to Meta di Sorrento.

Some of them, as previously stated, were in use until the 1950s and can be occasionally noticed amongst the vegetation or along the roadsides[3].

The old unit of measurement for lime was a bushel of 120 rolls, the equivalent of about one quintal.

150

Charcoal piles

Looking carefully, you might just be able to make out, under the trees or bushes, some of the tiny platforms serving charcoal burners to pile up the wood and assemble the ovens. During the autumn, on the Monti Lattari, hundreds of piles were built up to make coal from cut branches collected after the woods had been thinned out and the olive and other trees pruned. The stumps were stacked in the pile according to length. Smaller pieces were wrapped round the larger pieces, which made up the central core of fuel-wood, until they had formed a kind of cupola or dome about 2m in diameter and 1.6m high. This was in turn cov-ered with leaves and pieces of turf placed face down, with more soil piled on top. The oven was then lit from the top; a process often accompanied by prayers and good luck chants. The piles were then supposed to burn slowly and uniformly for five days and, as with lime, they were kept under surveillance day and night in case they caught fire or petered out. When the right amount of charring had been attained, the fire was smothered. The resulting fuel, duly sized up, was about a third of the initial weight of wood.

For weeks at a time, at dawn, long lines of people of any age and gender would walk down the mountain paths and around the village to distribute the fuel. Black all over

because of the dust that stuck to their sweaty bodies, they would all carry on their backs sacks of eight *cofani*[4] (baskets) which they managed to keep in place with the help of ropes and a *scapuccio*[5], with a handheld stick inserted in a rope loop and across the shoulder for increased stability. Most coal carriers did not have shoes or other suitable footwear and so used to wrap feet in sack-cloth as a protection from thorns and sharp stones. After the war, with the advent of bottled gas and electricity, this type of fuel production faded away.

[1] See footnote 11 on page 83.

[2] The chestnut, *Castanea sativa*, is a very old plant which has existed in the Mediterranean area since Cenozoic times. In the past, it was very important in the Italian diet because the dried fruit could be kept for unlimited time and could also be made into good quality flour, comparable, as to nutritional values, to wheat flour, which could save people from starvation when times were hard, before they started growing potatoes. In medieval times, Germanic peoples referred to chestnuts as "the Italian bread" and to the tree as a bread tree. In addition to the fruit, the chestnut tree provided other useful materials: the branches to make pergolas and the leaves as bedding for the animals in stables as well as for lining and covering the snow pits on the slopes of the Lattari mountains for summertime ice quarrying.

[3] For further information see *La produzione della calce nella Penisola sorrentino-amalfitana*, in "Le arti dell'acqua e del fuoco" published by the Centro di Cultura e Storia Amalfitana, 2004, pp. 215-61.

[4] The *cofano* was a basket, which also served as a unit of measurement, being the equivalent of about 10kg.

[5] A *scapuccio* was a kind of hat with a thick pad at the back of the neck, used to carry heavier loads on people's backs.

CHURCHES

The Chiesa Nuova quarter

Perched on a hilltop that offered natural protection against Saracen incursions, the Chiesa Nuova district formed when separate clusters of houses, built over the centuries around the ancient SS. Salvatore chapel, expanded and then merged. This chapel was one of the granges belonging to the Benedictine abbey of S. Vito e dell'Assunta, and the inhabited area surrounding it is one of the oldest in Positano.

Study of the irregular, yet consistent, urban fabric, and the sloping narrow streets around which the town grew over the centuries, leads to believe that the place dates back to around the year 1000. However, it is possible that there was an earlier settlement in this same place, because two Roman *cineraria* or ash-chests were found and then used as fonts in the sacristy at the Chiesa Nuova and in the nearby S. Lucia church.

In the past, only the precipitous steps of Via S. Giovanni provided access from this area to the rest of town and to the beach. Nowadays, the lowest part of this street is known as Via Trara Genoino.

In the 16th century three more towers were built inland to provide backup for the three coastal watch and defence towers against raids by assorted pirates and Turkish-Saracen corsairs. These can still be seen, even though entangled among new buildings.

In the past, this area was the site of a grange, linked directly to the abbey, as well as the now disappeared chapels of S. Lucia and S. Nicola, both on the path up to S. Maria del Castello. The Annunziata chapel was also here, but it was knocked down in

the second half of the 19th century to make room for the Amalfi-Meta di Sorrento road.

Of the ancient SS. Salvatore chapel, only the 16th century grey tuff portal remains, probably in its original shape, under the portico at the beginning of Via Mangialupini. A cross, carved on the trabeation, would seem to indicate that this portal was removed from a religious building.

The expression *miez'a terra*, meaning in the middle of the fields, is still used by the people of Positano to refer to the area between the State road and Viale Pasitea which leads down into the city centre, and confirms the existence of a grange run by

the Benedictine abbey, which owned the entire Positano territory anyway.

Even the agglomeration of houses called Pastiniello - which is a more modern area – must be considered as belonging to the Chiesa Nuova district. Its name, which is still used to refer to the S. Giovanni chapel, reminds us that much of the surrounding land, the property of either the abbey or the grange, had been leased out to peasants under a special contract termed *ad pastinandum*, which envisaged improvement to the land by planting (Latin *pastinare*) new trees, especially vines and olives[1].

Considering how many fortifications and inside towers were built in the surroundings

of the S. Giovanni church, this may be considered the only example of a fortified grange in our area (to the exclusion the Punta S. Elia grange which is protected by a tower-house) and maybe on the whole Amalfi coastline.

The Chiesa Nuova district was home to the aristocracy in the past: in its uppermost part survives a beautiful, well-preserved portal in grey tuff, which formed the entrance to a partially destroyed 18th-century villa. The coat of arms of the previous owners has been erased from the keystone in the arch – a normal practice when a property changed hands. This was one of many villas built during the town's finest period in the 18th century and probably belonged to some wealthy ship-

owner or church leader. The villa is, in fact, commonly known as La Casa dei Preti (the Priests' House). Along the old Via Fiume della Noce, which led to a spring now lying under the main road, there is another 18th-century portal, which would have been the entrance to another villa now completely destroyed. This one has the Buonocore family coat of arms on the keystone. The area was isolated and naturally protected from attack by outsiders until the end of the 18th century. Once the wide, easy stone steps known as Tese S. Giuseppe leading to S. Maria del Castello were built, and then the Meta-Amalfi road, the area was split up and much of its historical-cultural memory and identity was lost for ever.

The Chiesa Nuova

Lutheran reform and Protestantism cut the Northern European countries from the Church of Rome and overturned religious order there. In a bid to counter this situation, once the Council of Trent ended in 1563, the Church gave new impetus to religious architecture and sacred art, as both had an important role in enhancing people's faith. Religious fervour, expressed as a mass phenomenon in antithesis to the Reform, led for a long time many people across Catholic Europe to renovate or decorate their places of worship according to the dictates of the Council of Trent.

The tide reached Positano somewhat late, that is during the 18th century, when a lot of rebuilding and renovation work - prompted by the affluence attained by local trading and merchant families – was addressed to the religious buildings, and it was all done in the Baroque style. The erection, in the second half of this century, of the Chiesa Nuova on the site of the 11th-century SS. Sacramento chapel can be seen in such framework of events. Once construction works had been completed, the church was officially dedicated to the Madonna delle Grazie – but adroitly renamed Chiesa Nuova (New Church) by the townsfolk, a "practical" name, which has stuck for good.

Elliptical shape (with interior axes measuring 15.60m and 10.80m) and matching compartmented semi-ellipsoidal roof, make Chiesa Nuova one of the most interesting and important Baroque buildings in Positano and on the Amalfi coast. Along

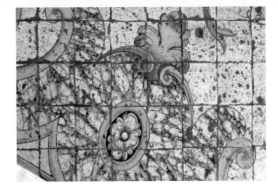

Previous page:
Interior decoration, Chiesa Nuova

Opposite:
Detail of a floor motif

Below:
Marble cherubs at the altar sides

with the Assunta church, it houses most of the town's artistic treasures and cultural heritage.

It is not known who built it, but similar architectural forms had already been adopted in Rome and Naples where there was a tradition of circular or elliptical religious buildings. Borromini in Rome and fra' Nuvolo in Naples were the most famous exponents of this new artistic trend[2]. The construction techniques, albeit on a much smaller scale, were the same as those used by the Romans for the Pantheon, and after it, for other circular buildings with spherical vaults. It is a technique which allows for the massive perimeter wall to be carved out to create extra spaces within its thickness as, in our case, five radial chapels, two entrances and the access to the sacristy.

The elliptical design was a sort of compromise between the central (or Greek cross) plan, and the longitudinal (or Latin cross) plan where, in Christian terms, the nave symbolizes the pathway to salvation and the cupola the Paradise above.

The main entrance, on the longer east-west axis, allows for an instant-perception and understanding of the inner architectural space. The visitor is immediately impressed by its shape, the paintings, the wonderful wall decoration and by how luminous it is. As you move inside, you embrace the whole structure, just as it embraces you.

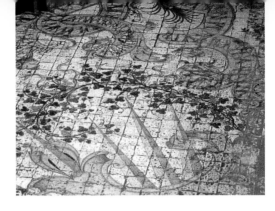

The arch-vaulted chapels around the ellipse are lower than the one housing the main altar, allowing it to stand out. The remarkable height of the supporting wall is mitigated by two cornices, featuring a mix of moulding and picture decoration, as well as by pilasters with composite capitals. The first section reaches to the height of the side chapels, the second, where there are three large windows lighting up the whole space, ends with a less fancy cornice upon which sits the imposing cupola.

The chapels are dedicated to S. Giuseppe, S. Alfonso de' Liguori (who maybe visited Positano), S. Michele, the SS. Annunziata and S. Pietro: they all have semicircular vaults and inlaid marble altars, decorated by precious, beautiful 18th-century canvases. There are two niches on either side of the main altar where wooden statues of the Madonna delle Grazie and the Redentore (the Redeemer) stand.

Apart from the main entrance on the median axis, there is another one, not far and smaller, facing the entrance to the sacristy. These unusually situated three doors meant that the congregation could better concentrate on prayer. The two holy water fonts of inlaid marble, on either side of the main door, were donated by the Montuori family.

The original, valuable coloured majolica floor is as interesting as it is beautiful.

It is a pity that down the middle and to the right, in line with the second entrance, the tiles are worn out because of so many people walking on them, and that the furniture resting on it only allows a partial view of this unique and wonderful work of art.

This floor depicts only one subject and is therefore one of the biggest of its kind. It bears comparison with its more famous counterparts, produced by the Neapolitan school led by the great master Ignazio Chiaiese, who worked at Capri a lot, and decorated the floor in the S. Michele Arcangelo church in Anacapri representing the Garden of Eden. He also did the S. Cataldo chapel in Massa Lubrense. Our floor is made of hand-decorated 20 x 20cm tiles. An elliptical frame set between the two foci of the ellipse features a pyx, which is almost illegible now. Dark and bright blue rays against a white background radiate from the frame towards the grape-bearing vines and green palm branches, both evangelical symbols, growing out from the golden yellow and orange border which encloses the artwork around the walls. The lack of any document attesting where the floor was made leaves us guessing about the artist and the master craftsmen who, as we will see later, also worked in other Positano churches during the same period. Given how similar the colour and design are to those of the church

of the S. Arcangelo in Cava de' Tirreni, it is possible that master craftsmen from Cava or Vietri did the work, as both places were famous for their artistry in majolica tile production.

The inside of the elliptical dome has geometric decorations in relief, which look like (or actually are) structural ribs. These grow out from the pillars and mount towards the centre to meet an elliptical inset reflecting the one on the floor. A stucco ostensory surrounded by cherubs decorates it. The light that comes in from the high windows is discreet and charming. A high source of light in a church also has symbolic and esoteric value in the religious ritual: the immaterial nature of the light mirrors that of faith.

The altar in S. Giuseppe chapel, the first on the right as one moves in, is bare and plain compared to the other Baroque altars because, as a carved stone at its base reminds us, it was remade in 1893. The painting in the masonry frame above the altar shows the Holy Family and bears an inscription with the names of the benefactors and painter. But the pre-existing frame being smaller than the canvas, the same had to be folded round the edges in a way that the inscription cannot be read in its entirety.

The altar in the S. Alfonso chapel, the next one, is also made of inlaid marble, and has a 1775 devotional inscription, also in Latin, by a "Michele Russo and his sailors".

The main altar, of inlaid marble as the Baroque tradition dictates, stands inside a somewhat larger chapel. At its base a 1768 inscription states that it was commissioned by "Filippo Attanasio and his sailors". This date means that the church was actually built slightly earlier than reported by both Talamo (1890) and Vespoli (1775). A picture, in a niche above, shows the adoration of the Madonna delle Grazie. The relevant dedication says it was donated by someone bearing the Talamo family name.

The other two altars on the left also are in inlaid marble and, at the base of the S. Michele altar, there is a 1775 inscription

replicating that by the Attanasio mentioned above.

The altar in the S. Pietro chapel is the same as the others, but there is neither a dedication nor the name of the person who commissioned or donated it.

Above the entrance is a *cantorìa* (upper floor gallery or tribune – usually furnished with an organ – as wide as the main nave and overlooking the church interior from above the entrance) whose organ was donated, as the plaque on the wooden balustrade tells us, again in 1775, by the same "Filippo Attanasio and his sailors". It is clear from all these dedications that the church was completely renovated during the second half of the 18th century by ship-owners and sailors who maybe lived in the area, along with significant contributions from a devout Filippo Attanasio. The

walls are all decorated and divided by pilaster strips with composite capitals, which makes this church interior a particularly beautiful single space. In 1846 the Archbishop of Amalfi entrusted the church to the Congregazione dei Perpetui Adoratori (Confraternity of the Perpetual Worshippers) who founded the contiguous convent, run by the Suore della Carità. In 1866 the convent was closed down by the new Italian State and, three years later, it was turned over to the Positano Municipality.

In the sacristy a Roman marble *cinerarium* (ash-chest), now built into the wall, but once utilized elsewhere as a font (a spigot still protrudes from the front side), was described by Vittorio Bracco[3] as a marble box 24.5cm high, 45cm wide, about 28cm deep. "On the front side, under the cartouche, a garland hangs from the horns

of two rams in the corners. Two sparrows peck at the fruit beneath the garland. The other sides, also decorated with fruit and vegetal decoration, are partly walled in".

The Latin inscription in the cartouche translates as follows: "To Actis, [son] of Caesar, [who] lived 36 years".

The fact that such archaeological remains were appropriated and used for different purposes is highly criticized today, but their being salvaged this way has meant that part of our historical and artistic heritage was not lost forever.

Two stairways lead up from the sacristy, the first to the organ, and the other to a mezzanine floor lighted by a small window opening on the side of the churchyard. A small door to the right of the altar leads to the monastery.

The outside, in stark contrast with the inside, has practically no decoration. There is a graceful campanile to the side of the passageway linking church and monastery.

At the back of the churchyard, in a small niche facing the main entrance, there is an old wooden cross, now rather worn by an unknown artist.

Not far away lies the S. Lucia chapel, the former church of the Trinity. Another Roman ash-chest was housed in the sacristy here and Errico Talamo described it as follows: "the most beautiful of these [ash-chests] was the one in the S. Lucia sacristy, used for exactly the same purpose [as that in Chiesa Nuova]. It showed a woman lying in the water and unfolding a veil. This urn was purloined and sold to an Englishman".

Further up, along the Tese S. Giuseppe leading to S. Maria del Castello, there was the chapel of S. Nicola, but, as with many other chapels, nothing remains of it except the memory of where it stood.

The Church of S. Giovanni

Going down the old steps in Via San Giovanni, which led from Chiesa Nuova to the main beach, once past the Viale Pasitea and the Villa Franca Hotel, one comes to the S. Giovanni chapel, formerly called the S. Giovanni de Pastinello *or* Trabucco[4]. The word Pastinello recalls the *pastinato*, the oldest and most common type of agricultural contract for tillage and management of agricultural land.

The chapel is made up of a fairly small room having a barrel-vaulted ceiling with lunettes and windows only on the seaside wall, against which leans a lower room acting as sacristy. Apart from the stucco decoration (which in poorer communities substituted for marble and sculptures), different from that of the other churches in Positano, original features of this church are represented by an interesting tile floor, a precious altar frontal, and a Roman cinerarium built into the sacristy wall.

The floor is part Campanian terracotta and part majolica, a technique adopted by the Vietri master tilers. It depicts a wind rose in memory of the renovation work carried out by don Antonio Romito in 1850.

The altar frontal, and the decorated fascia above it and extending on both sides of the tabernacle, are unique to Positano. They were most likely taken from another church and brought here after the don Romito renovation. The frontal, which is slightly smaller than the old

altar it is attached to, does not completely cover the older decorated surface. The idea that it came from a different church is also supported by the central figure of S. Antonio (rather than S. Giovanni). The wonderful composition of flower decoration, Renaissance spirals and grotesque volutes used as perches by exotic birds, was made using a technique which was fashionable at the time in Neapolitan art workshops[5].

It was Talamo again, when talking about the various churches that have been lost or converted, who mentions a "chapel of S. Antonio at the house where Samuele Attanasio dwells". This was a private chapel and it is highly probable that the altar decorative piece came from there.

On the altar, a fine Baptism of Christ painting is in awful conditions, and risks being lost forever because of leaking rainwater, rising damp and the general state of neglect of the place.

The dedication to S. Giovanni Battista, the wind rose on the floor and especially the altar covering, all lead to believe that this church was founded by a member of the Order of the Hospital of St. John of Jerusalem, or in memory of another member belonging to the same Order, founded by fra' Gerardo Sasso di Scala (near Ravello) to help pilgrims on their way to the Holy Land.

On the front wall of the sacristy an ancient Roman ash-chest, once used as a font, is built into the wall. It shows a young man whose body is being laid to rest by two

Previous page:
The high altar, Church of S. Giovanni
Below:
Detail of its tiled roof

other men and it might as well depict the deposition of Christ. However, since it is walled in, it is impossible to know what other scenes, if any, appear on the other sides, though they would almost certainly be decorated.

Vittorio Bracco ventured into a passionate – if a bit far on the side of imagination – account of this object:

"A white marble rectangular-shaped urn (28cm high, 35cm wide, 29cm deep) [is] *built into the sacristy of the little church of S. Giovanni Battista. The inscription would have been on the lid, like the Furore* [between Positano and Amalfi] *urn. The front side shows a young man being laid to the ground by two men who are holding him,* one at the feet and the other at the shoulders. These men are probably libitinarii or undertakers, but their faces have completely faded. The features of the other four people in the scene are also unrecognisable. One man is kneeling down to give the young man a last kiss and is probably the father, and another figure standing behind him with right hand on chin could be the mother. Two other people have their back to the group. One of them has the right arm in the air as if maybe carrying a lantern, and the other one is so badly worn that you can only see his bearded head, covered by his hood. This couple, whose posture is vaguely reminiscent of [the ceremonial linked to] a priest taking the dead away, will probably

Previous page:
High altar canvas, Battesimo di Cristo
Below:
More details of the altar frontal

lead the group to the ustrinum, *where the body will be cremated. It cannot be excluded that the hidden sides of the urn were likewise decorated. To be noticed is the unnatural position of the corpse's right arm, which does not hang dead like the other one but is laid on his head as if he was asleep, which was the custom at the time.*

What does not need pointing out, because it strikes the observer immediately, is how similar the whole composition is to a Deposition of Christ we associate with Renaissance Christian iconography, as with Donatello and Raphael: the close-knit group, the way the deceased body lies, the grief that is still tangible as one man bends over and another figure is holding back the tears. And it is almost certain that this iconography is based on carvings from Greek and Imperial age urns, especially those depicting the carrying away of Meleagros' body[6] (…) Although there is

very little to go on, especially because the expressions and details, such as the folds in the vestments, have almost completely disappeared, I would say the urn is to be probably dated to the late II century, Severan age – also on account of the way the figures are contained and almost flattened within the scene, not to mention a kind of overall roughness" [7].

The seeping rainwater and damp are causing irreparable damage to this most valuable ash-chest as well. If no action is taken soon, it may well be too late and the whole thing will disintegrate.

There is no significant external decoration in the S. Giovanni church except the frames outlining the gable and the cornice on top the entrance portal. The sparingly ornamented façade can be explained away considering its location: Via S. Giovanni is too narrow for people to step back and catch sight of the whole building.

Below the terrace providing access to the villa opposite the church, there are the remains of a tower and a larger 16th-century defence system, now incorporated into a more modern building. The system was probably only armed with guns because the Spanish governors at the time did not allow privately-managed inland forts to have cannons, fearing that in a popular uprising the guns might be turned against them. These strongholds were built to defend the grange and the road leading to the shore. Their size leads to believe that they accounted for the "Positano castle" mentioned by the Turkish admiral Piri Reis in his logbook.

Behind the church there are other remains, which could have belonged to the same complex or possibly to another inland tower.

The Church of S. Matteo

Down from Chiesa Nuova, once to Viale Pasitea intersection, a left turn to Via Monte takes to the little church of S. Matteo. This is rectangular in shape with a barrel-vaulted ceiling and, as an inscription in the beautiful floor reminds us, it was renovated in 1797. Further restoration work was carried out in 1897, as stated in a second inscription. The walls are decorated with stucco relief work and pilaster strips. A first inspection of the architectural design leads to the assumption that the renovation work was carried out by the same group of artists, decorators and master masons who were working in Positano at the time. Above the keystones in the arches, stucco cherubs, similar to those in the central nave in the Assunta church and the Santa Margherita church, unfold their wings. The same goes for the pseudo-composite capitals on the pilaster strips. Some of the stucco decoration on the altar has come off.

Left of the entrance, there is a shell-shaped red porphyry Holy Water font built into the wall.

Until the last century there was also an ancient marble plaque here, which maybe came from the Positano Roman villa, depicting a man with a basket of fruit surrounded by bagpipe players. It is now housed in the National Archaeological Museum in Naples.

The chapel faces on to the tight steps (*scalinatella*) of Via Monte, so has no external decoration apart from an arched structure surmounting the gable, with a little bell in it.

Rainwater keeps seeping in through the brickwork and, in combination with rising damp, causes the floor to break up and a lot of the precious stucco work to crumble.

This church, like that of San Giovanni, or perhaps even more so, is in serious danger of collapse.

Previous page:
Rosary Church, doorway detail
Below:
Roman sarcophagus with the myth of Bacchus

The Church of the Rosario

Carrying on towards the beach, once at Punta Reginella, Viale Pasitea will take you to Piazzetta dei Mulini, where the Church of the Rosario stands. This is the only church with a west-facing altar, and it is the only surviving part of the old monastery of the Padri Domenicani, whose devotion to the Rosary is well known. The complex of buildings extended all around and below the current street level before the landslide that made the tuff cliff collapse into the Valle Pozzo river destroyed most of it, along with the art treasures it housed.

The church has one nave subdivided into compartments and a presbitery-apse two steps higher up.

After the latest restoration work a few years ago, only the burial stone of abbot Giovanni Andrea De Palma has been left on the floor. Underneath the family insignia, it has the following inscription in Lat-in: *"To Giovanni Andrea De Palma, son of Geronimo, an extremely right and kind man, who, after being appointed abbot of the monastery, even though he had to leave Naples, and his still-living father, to move here, never forgot his birth place. Grateful, he ordered his brethren to bury him in this place. The De Palma brothers, sons of Raffaele, his heirs, did as he asked. He died on 28 December 1620 at age 75"*.

On the wall to the left of entrance there is another stone plaque with the following inscription: *"Emiddio Savino, sated with good luck in America and progeny in his country, here came to rest, aged 70, on 7 June 1881.* [This epigraph was] *laid by his disconsolate wife and children"*.

These mementos and a Roman sarcophagus depicting the myth of Bacchus on the front panel, are the only remaining witnesses to a former magnificence. The origins of this church have been forgotten over time. We know that in 1614 it was donated by the

Previous page:
La Madonna del Rosario with S. Domenico and S. Rosa da Lima

Opposite:
Fresco with the Madonna

Below:
Altar piece and old photo of the Rosary Church

Town Council, along with some estates and revenues, to the Dominican Fathers, so that they could set up a monastery to teach people some religion. The monastery was built to the left of the church but it was closed down in 1652 by Pope Innocence X under a ruling that suppressed, all over the Catholic world, the monasteries that had not enough monks and/or resources, whereupon it was used as a court of justice. Once the tuff cliff that the monastery stood on collapsed, as is demonstrated by all the partially buried walls below ground level today, most of the treasures were lost and the church was deconsecrated. A century later, the building was renovated by don Mariano Talamo and people started to worship there again, becoming the seat of the SS. Rosario Congregation.

The presbitery-apse is topped by a drum and cupola with a blind tuff lantern on top. On the right wall, in the first section of the nave, there is a picture of the Madonna and, in the second one, since 2006, an 18th-century canvas of the Madonna del Rosario with S. Domenico and S. Rosa da Lima, by the Piedmontese painter Giuseppe Bianchi, which was donated by Attilio Alessandro Bollini.

Worthy of note are the main gable and the side door, both in grey tuff with bas-relief decoration. To the right of the entrance, a composite capital and other things taken from the 17th-century façade of the Mother Church (Chiesa dell'Assunta) form the base for a black cross which marks the missions of the Padri Passionisti.

197

Previous page:
Via dei Mulini

Opposite:
Panorama, early 1900s

Below:
Century-old *Wisteria* vine in Via della Teglia

The Parish Church of the Assunta

Walking along Via dei Mulini which leads down to the beach, one gets to the Chiesa Madre or Assunta Church which was always the centre of religious life in Positano, and was both its symbol and most famous monument. Here is the revered Byzantine icon of the Black Madonna and other treasures, including a splendid wooden statue of a Madonna with Child. Built on the ruins of the old S. Vito and S. Maria Assunta abbey church, it has been renovated and extended over the centuries to make it look as it does today. It was originally founded by Basilian monks from the East in the 8th century, and had a Greek-cross plan. A parchment held by the Parish archives details how the church was dedicated to the Blessed Virgin Mary by the Bishop of Amalfi, Giovanni II, in 1159.

In 1777, when the building was on the verge of collapse, the Commendatory Abbots removed all the treasures and expensive furnishings. These included the African breccia columns which the monks from the SS. Trinità in Naples had given them, the red porphyry holy water font, and an altar in "antique green" marble which were moved to the cathedral in Amalfi in exchange for the two cast iron lions which stand at either side of the stairway leading from the beach up to the church. The lions were made to decorate a fountain which was never finished. All trace and record of the many other treasures that fired the

hearts of the faithful have been lost. Errico Talamo described it like this: "This church is 140 palms long, and 84 wide (35x20m). It is designed according to the Greek-cross plan. The roof was once held up by huge timber beams with piperno supports to the sides. The walls were decorated with antique green marble slabs and with columns of Egyptian granite, antique green, and African breccia. The floor was covered in beautiful mosaics. It only had one door".

Some wretched remains of the antique mosaic floor are still visible behind the new altar, while the columns from the nave are scattered all over the town. When the church was rebuilt, and made bigger, its plan changed to a Latin cross, with three naves and three entrances. The marble columns used as decoration pieces in the church-yard, in Piazzetta Amerigo Vespucci and at the entrance to the Galeone (an old access road to the church, now covered), as well as those serving as seats in the churchyard until the 1950s, all came from the old church - although, before that, they were taken from the old Roman villa when the first abbey church was built. Rather questionable renovation work, carried out in 1926, covered all trace of the old façade with its pilaster strips and architraves in grey tuff. Only a few pilasters and capitals survived and can be found in the sacristy now, along with a few other bits and pieces lying untended around the town.

Whereas the old façade was the same height as the line of the church roof ridge,

Previous page:
Assunta Church from the beach

Below:
Votive images of Madonna Assunta, the one to the left painted by Vincenzo Caprile

the new one is ten metres higher and so rises higher than the campanile, overshadowing it. It detracts from the historic significance and importance of the campanile because, when seen from certain angles, the excessively high prospect sort of pushes the campanile out of the foreground. Another even more serious consequence of this clumsy work is that the splendid cupola has been hidden behind this nondescript wall so that its majesty, importance and intrinsic value as a cityscape element are lost in an altogether different perception of the whole picture.

The higher façade is also out of proportion with the small churchyard, whose later renovation only served to emphasize how the old harmony of style and composition between the churchyard, the church and the campanile had been broken, making those same elements to appear disparate and conflicting.

The only photo of the old façade shows it to be vaguely reminiscent of that of S. Gennaro church in Vettica di Praiano. When the organ was taken out at the beginning of the current century to be replaced with the new one, some tuff decorations came to light. The church has a Latin-cross plan, with

MIRACOLOSA IMMAGINE DI MARIA SS. DI POSITANO

DECORATA DELLA CORONA D'ORO

three naves, transept, vaulted semi-circular apse and two side-chapels. The naves are subdivided by five arches supported by pillars which, it is said, surround ancient columns[8]. The main nave, built by Sicilian craftsmen, has a barrel vault, sided with lunettes. Light comes in from large windows beneath the lunettes. There are stucco figures on the keystones, and pseudo-Ionic capitals adorn the pilaster strips, with floral decorations hanging from them.

The side naves are lower and covered with segmental cupolas. There are four arch-vaulted chapels on each side with altars in inlaid marble. The 18th-century paintings above the altars show that they are dedicated to S. Biagio, the Immaculate Conception,

S. Antonio and S. Anna. Most of the altars were donated by *"Luca and Giomarino Buonocore and their sailors"* in 1781. At the fifth arch there is the opening to the sacristy. Along the left nave are the chapels with pictures of S. Nicola di Bari attributed to Solimena, S. Vito and S. Maria delle Grazie, the Annunciation, the Crucifixion and, where the last arch rises, there is the entrance from Via della Teglia. A sculpted gilt-wood coat of arms of the town of Positano crowns the triumphal arch.

Where the nave meets the transept, on a drum unusually tall, stands the cupola. It is a lofty, majestic, gusseted structure, the most imposing on the whole Amalfi coast. This is the real symbol of Positano.

Gaetanus Caporano F. 1784

206

207

FORTUNATUS ET BONAVENTURA FRATRES
MILIANO FIERI CURARUNT A·D·1795·

208

DOMINICUS
ATTANASIO
FIERI CURAVIT
A.D. 1708

In the apse is the inlaid marble altar, on top of which stands the decorative shrine, a splendid example of Neapolitan baroque, sheltering the precious icon of the Black Madonna with the Blessing Child, painted on Lebanese cedar boards and measuring 1.20m x 2.30m.

From the 12th century onwards, Byzantine icons which were more than 1m high started to be made, and only Christ and the Madonna were shown facing the viewer, while the apostles and other saints were always shown in profile. The Positano icon is different from its contemporaries because the Madonna is sitting on the throne, which is very unusual, has a rich tunic and mantle and wears a crown. Her right hand touches her blessing son on the shoulder in a protective gesture. The gilt background, which gradually replaced the blue of the older icons, became popular from 11th century onwards.

The Madonna and child's faces were not black to start with, but the oxidation of the paint within the ageing process has made them undergo this change[9]. The shrine – four pink granite columns, the front ones supporting the gable, with two angels on top holding up a golden crown – was made

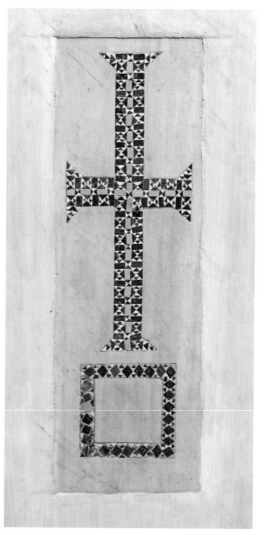

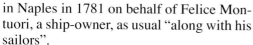

PYRRVS IŌĒS CAMPĻIS NEAP͛ͨ
QVI ANNO·M·D·LX CᴀNONICVS
PᴀRTHENOPEIÆ Ecc͛ CREᴀTVS
ᴀNO VERO·M·D·LXXXVI Ab ͱͱͱ· D͂NO
Cᴀʀᴅ·S͆͆͆· SEVERINE PROTHONOTARI͛
Λʀᴏ· ET POSĪTANI Abbas
Fᴀᴄᴛvs Fviᴛ
N CVIVS MEMORIA HÆG POSVIT·M·D͞

in Naples in 1781 on behalf of Felice Montuori, a ship-owner, as usual "along with his sailors".

There are different versions of the *posa posa*, the legend relating to the arrival of this icon in Positano. One says that it came to our shores following the iconoclasm decreed by the Emperor of the Orient Leone III Isaurico in 725-726; another that it had been stolen, though it is not said from where, in a Saracen raid: when the boat carrying the icon got to Positano, the raiders heard a mysterious voice telling them *posa posa* (meaning "put it down": obviously it was a case of Saracens being cognizant of the Italian language) and they were so scared they turned tail and fled, leaving the statue on the shore. Apart from the legend and its various interpretations, what is interesting is the fervent devotion shown by people – not only from Positano – for the Black Madonna. When the painting was restored in the Capodimonte Museum workshop in the 1950s, it was dated to the beginning of 13th century.

Against the sidewalls of the choir stand the carved wooden stalls. There is a niche at both the transept ends of the choir, one with a statue of the Addolorata and one of Christ tied to the column, made by Michele Trilocco

213

in 1798. It gives comfort to see some artistic gems that somehow managed to escape the raids of the… commendatory abbots.

On the left side of the arch, leading from the right nave into the transept, there is a memorial stone to Pirro Giovanni Campoliso, abbot of Positano, with the bishops' insignia, the campanile, and the following Latin inscription: "*Pirro Giovanni Campoliso became a canon of the Neapolitan Church in the year 1586, and was made protonotary and abbot of Positano in 1586 by the most illustrious Cardinal of S. Severina. This stone was placed here in 1600 to mark the event*".

To the right is the marble reliquary of S. Vito, a precious 1506 Renaissance piece by the maestro Giovan Tommaso Malvito, commissioned, as reported in the inscription below, by Bernardo De Palma. Another Neapolitan School piece from the same period, by Francesco Laurana, is a gilt copper bust of S. Vito with a silver head, placed, along with the wooden statue of the Madonna of Positano, in the chapel to the right of the presbitery. There is an oval on the bust's chest with the Latin inscription "To S. Vito, Protector of Positano", while another, in the same language, on the bust's base, says: "Filippo III reigning, this work was commissioned and paid for by the Confraternita del Monte del Corpo di Cristo. Its governors, Onorato Porzio, A. and M.D., Marco Aurelio D'Urso, Silvestro Mirella and Domenico

SACELLVM HOC, QVOD CÔSTRVÉDVM, ET
CIRCVCISIONI DICÃDVM NICOLAVS IOÃES DE VRSO
LEGAVIT, HÆREDES EI9 EFFICIENDV CVRARVNT 1599

216

217

Romito - under the pontificate [1592-1605] of Clemente VIII".

Light comes into this chapel from a glass window with floral designs made at the end of 19th century and donated, as it can be read at the bottom, by Roberto and Maria Priore De Pirro, descendants of the same family to which the famous abbot Pirro Giovanni Campoliso also belonged.

The chapel on the left is that of the SS. Sacramento.

The church also displays a host of fine 17th-century Neapolitan School paintings. On the altar in the right arm of the transept is the Circoncisione, an impressive and valuable work of art from 1599, attributed to Fabrizio Santafede. It echoes a more famous Circumcision the painter and architect Marco Pino did for the Church of the Jesuits in Naples,

and also that by Giovan Bernardo Lama, in the church of S. Luca in Praiano. On the altar, to the left of the apse, hangs the 16th-century Madonna del Carmine which was donated by the Calabrian Certosa of Santo Stefano del Bosco in Serra San Bruno.

Two 15th-century marble crosses with inlaid decoration, salvaged from the earlier church, are walled into the inner side of the pillars of the triumphal arch.

Above the entrance is the *cantorìa* built in the 1950s to replace the old wooden one, which had become unstable. A monumental new organ welcomed the Third Millennium with its inaugural concert.

In the sacristy, there are several paintings to admire, including the Cristo con la Croce, commissioned by a Confraternity and recently restored on behalf of

TROVANDOSI QUESTO BRIGANTINO SOPRO I BANCHI D'INGLITERRA CIRCA 10
MIGLIA A MARE. SI MISE UNA ORAGANA TEMPESTA CORRENTE A DESCRIZION
DEL TEMPO, CHE SI BURAVA 6 ALTRE ORE DI QUESTA TEMPESTA ERAVAMO TUT
TI PERDUTI ACCADUTO LI 2 DICEMBRE 1863. V.F.G.A.

1 AGOSTO 1810. IL SIG: D. GIUSEPPE ROSSI AVENDO NOLEGGIATO
UNA BARCA PER PORTARSI IN MESSINA FU SORPRESO DA FORTE
TEMPESTA CON VENDO DI PONENTO E MAESTRO FUORI STRONBOLI

Poi fatto grazia finita il 23 Dicembre 1882. Cofrilano Delesere Giovanni

V.F.G.A.

220

Italian-American Major General Antony J. Carrano; an old 12th- or 13th-century painting on a wooden stand showing the dedication of the church to the Madonna Assunta, as well as several votive paintings from sailors miraculously saved in rough seas. In the first chapel to the left, dedicated to S. Nicola, a permanent crèche with valuable 18th-century statuettes has been set out.

There are still remains of the original decoration, like the side naves windows' tuff piers and gables, the pilasters and capitals of the cupola drum, as well as other bits and pieces from the 18th-century structure, which help to understand what the building must have originally looked like. From the outside, the majestic ribbed cupola, topped by a windowed lantern, is decorated in green, blue and white majolica geometric patterns.

221

The Oratory Chapel

The ancient Congrega della Buona Morte (Brotherhood of the Peaceful Death) in Positano chose to join forces with the Rome section of the same association in 1640, so as to benefit from the same privileges and rights. Although it is not known exactly when the Positano Chapter was founded, it is positive that their meeting place was originally the chapel to the left of the central nave in the Chiesa Madre. This chapel was torn down in 1771 to make room for one of the two side naves in the new church.

The new chapel was built a little further up, but still alongside the church, over the old abbey cemetery. It has one nave and a semi-circular apse with a large wooden crucifix and statues of the Madonna and S. Giovanni on either side of it. Talamo says that the 15m x 6m barrel-vaulted ceiling was coloured and maybe frescoed, but nothing remains of its old decoration or colour.

Until a few years ago the wooden benches around the walls used for the Brotherhood's assemblies could be seen. There is a *cantorìa* with organ above the main entrance.

Although some "maintenance" work has been done over the years, like removing the pews, altar and floor, fortunately the original late 18th-century façade has not changed. Its pilasters and pseudo-capitals, though in stucco, and the decorations, similar to the tuff ones in the Chiesa Madre, have survived – so they help us to figure out what the Chiesa Madre façade would have looked like in earlier times.

There is a painting in the church by the Russian exile Vassilij Necitailov, locally known as "*don Basilio*", who lived in Positano for a time. It shows the arrival here of the Black Madonna. Some of the faces of the people gathered to watch the event are recognisable as belonging to people living in Positano during the 1950s, when the painting was made.

224

Page 223:
Façade and high altar pieces of Oratorio chapel

Previous page:
Madonna di Positano

Below:
Paintings preserved in the Oratorio chapel

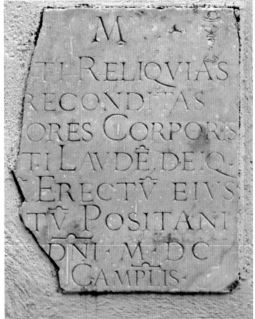

The Lapidarium, *or Epigraphs' Exhibit*

At the end of Via dei Mulini, before the ramp leading up to the Chiesa Madre churchyard, is Via della Teglia, which skirts the outer wall of the left-hand nave of the church. The name "Teglia" does not come from the *Tilia europaea* or lime-tree which stands on the overlying slope, but derives from a Greek word meaning "covered part". Maybe it had to do with Saracen incursions and a rolling-shutter (*saracinesca* in Italian) protection against them.

Along the outside wall of the left nave unfolds the collection of tombstones that used to be in the church, as well as Roman remains incorporated into the structure. On one of the tombstones the surname Mirella[i], one of the oldest and most prominent families in Posi-

tano, can still be read. On another is the name Galterius, and on a stone fragment the name of the abbot (?) Campanile, who held the post in 1586 according to the plaque in the church.

Another plaque fragment records the commitment of the unnamed friar who campaigned to get the campanile built. Talamo recorded the whole Latin inscription, before about half of it got lost. "D.O.M. [*Domini Omnipotentis Misericordia*, or by the mercy of the omnipotent God] - This campanile was built from its foundations in 1707 thanks to the promotion and cooperation of a Capuchin monk, donations from Christians and the devotion of the population and the clergy".

There are, also embedded in the wall, some remains from the Roman villa.

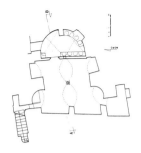

The crypt

Further on, underneath the portico, a room has recently been opened up to allow people access to the crypt, which extends under the transept and choir-apse. Some experts say that these reflect features the of the ancient abbey church. Over the last few years, the crypt has gradually been dug out and now two naves with barrel-vaulted ceilings can be seen, as well as an apse that was converted into a cemetery for the monks from the abbey when the church was no longer used. An old legend says that an icon of the Madonna was found here on top of a bush of myrtle, and this was the sign that a church should be built in her honour in this place. The stone chairs where the corpses of influential members of the clergy were seated and tied to the wall can be "admired" here[10]. A staircase connecting the two churches was closed, while the upper church was renovated, by the means of a beautifully decorated marble slab, perhaps an altar's frontal.

Inside, to allow the cupola to be adequately supported, the structure was reinforced with massive pillars girdling the original granite columns, so that only two of these remain in view.

The campanile

To the left of the churchyard towers the majestic campanile which was built in 1707 thanks to money collected by a Capuchin monk as detailed in the memorial stone previously described. It has four storeys with corner pilasters, window-frames and mouldings to outline the different floors, all in grey tuff. Before being removed in the 1950s, a marble-faced large clock, along with bells in an arched structure on the roof, marked the time. An ancient white marble stone, which used to be part of the church floor, has been built into the campanile face, just above the entrance door. It shows a sea monster, as Matteo Camera claims, surrounded by seven fish and an animal that looks like a fox. This was the old (11th- 12th- century) presbyterial barrier in the ancient abbey, and remained in the church until 1881 when the campanile was restored.

Other people say it symbolises the Sirens and thus death. Above this, a marble inscription, erected in 1902 on the occasion of the 600th anniversary of the invention of the compass, is a reminder of the legendary Positano origins of Flavio Gioia. The upper floors have arched windows all around, and the last level is

231

where the bells, now electronically run, are housed. To the left of the campanile, built into the garden wall of the house above, is a memorial plaque dedicated to the people of Positano who died in the last wars.

At the entrance to the churchyard stand two old marble columns, found when the church was rebuilt. They rise at the top of the majestic limestone steps leading up from the beach through Piazzetta del Saracino to the churchyard. To the right of the first landing, there is a niche with an 18th-century picture of the Pietà con la Maddalena (the deposition of Christ with Mary of Magdala), as well as the remains of a mosaic decoration on a marble slab, which were salvaged from the rubble of the old church. The steps are so grand and imposing that it is easy to surmise that this was the main access to the church and abbey before Via dei Mulini was opened.

If we carry on, we will see that at the sides of the twin ramps of the stairway there is a column and a stone corbel placed vertically, with a cobra head carved on the front and two birds on the sides. It is unknown where it came from or what period it was.

In the space between the two ramps there is an artistic fountain, built in 1881 and decorated with a terracotta cupid, which was stolen in the 1980s.

The Fornillo Area
and the Church of S. Margherita

Up Viale Pasitea or the other steps departing from the topmost section of the Chiesa Nuova district, it is possible to reach Fornillo, a 16th- or 17th-century settlement. Its entrance is marked by a natural cave, inside which there is a votive shrine and a crib scene with typical miniature Positano houses.

Thanks to local volunteers, at Christmas time the area is floodlighted and comes to life in a charming way. The name Fornillo is not, as popular tradition would have it, because in this place there was a small bread oven supplying Emperor Tiberius who, when he stayed at Capri, always had his bread made in Positano for fear of being poisoned: the name again comes from the Greek, and means reed or cane, a plant which still grows along the Fiume della Noce valley and behind the beach of the same name, where it was used in the past by local fishermen to make baskets and fish traps.

Fornillo has always been a refuge and a place of relaxation for artists and writers, be they Italians or foreigners. Among its inhabitants we can list painters, like Vincenzo Caprile, whose villa is still extant, Mauritius Cornelis Escher, Massimo Campigli, Raffaele Bella, and writers such as playwright Giulio Cesare Viola, dramatist, director and screenwriter Aldo Di Benedetto – plus a vast assortment of other relevant creative personalities.

Previous page:
Fornillo

Opposite:
Fornillo, by Anita Rée

Below:
Torre di Fornillo or del Germano

Down the ramps leading from Fornillo to the beach is the tiny church of S. Margherita, rectangular in plan, with a single barrel-vaulted nave, with lunettes, two side-altars and the sacristy to the left. Above the entrance is the *cantorìa* with a derelict organ.

Built by the Porcelli family, perhaps in 16th or 17th century, it was restored in the second half of the 18th century by people of the area with a contribution from Nicola Romito, as reported by a stone plaque in Latin built into the main façade: "This temple, dedicated to the Virgin S. Margherita and to the Martyrs of this royal town of Positano, which lay in ruins for a long time, was renovated by the Porcelli family as an act of devotion and at their own expenses, and by the citizens of the lower district of Fornillo as an act of devotion and also with the collaboration of Nicola Romito son of the late Pietro".

Shorter devotional inscriptions, dating to 1790 and 1791, can be read even at

the base of the high and side altars, which are all in inlaid marble. In a niche above the high altar is a statue of S. Margherita. Other works of art in this small temple include statuettes with the Archangel Raffaele, S. Margherita and the Addolorata.

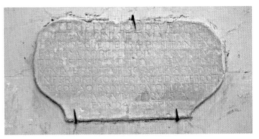

The Campanian terracotta floor, with majolica insets decorated with flower patterns similar to those in the Chiesa Nuova, is of a superior quality. It can be assumed that when the renovation and restoration work was carried out on most of the churches in Positano at the end of the 18th century, all the floors were commissioned from the same workshop. We can also infer that, since the stucco works and internal decoration here, and at the church of San Matteo, are similar to that of the Assunta church, the same master decorators must have executed them all.

The Church of S. Caterina

Along Viale Pasitea, not far from the Fornillo cave, stands a Neo-gothic chapel dedicated to S. Caterina.

According to tradition, the Porcelli family founded it, but Talamo says that merchants from Positano had it built because they had trade links with Egypt, especially the city of Alexandria where this revered saint had performed many miracles or obtained them through her intercession. It is possible that the two stories coincide because the Porcelli family, one of the wealthiest and most famous in Positano, accumulated much of their wealth thanks to the shipping trade, so it is very likely that this family, like many others, had business interests in Alexandria.

In the 18th century the church was in terrible condition, and in danger of collapse. Renovation work was undertaken by the Cinque family, one of the richest and most prominent in the district, and maybe they made it bigger than it was before.

In the 1920s, to make way for the construction of Viale Pasitea the church was

partly demolished, and promptly rebuilt in pseudo-gothic style by the local inhabitants because they did not want to lose their own church. During this round of works, the old flagstone floor was replaced with terracotta tiles.

This is the smallest of the Positano chapels, with only one nave and ceiling with pointed arches. In the apse, above the main altar, is a small window: along with pseudo-gothic side-windows, they flood the place with light. The chapel measures 13m x 5m, and to the right of it there is the small rectangular vestry.

Above this, a tiny, slim bell-tower completes the work.

In a niche carved into the back wall, above the inlaid marble high altar, stands the miraculous statue of S. Caterina. A second inlaid marble altar, on the left side-wall, is dedicated to the Sacro Cuore.

These 18th-century altars are all that remain of the rich décor which gradually disappeared as the church was renovated. Worthy of note are the short ramp and the access portal that, during the latest restoration work, were done in crafted limestone.

Previous page:
Liparlati, as seen from Palazzo Murat

Opposite:
Liparlati, by Ivan Zagoruiko

Below:
Liparlati in an old photo (1899)

The Liparlati District

Perched on the edge of the steep Monte ridge which offered it natural protection from enemy attacks, Liparlati, whose borders are formed by the Valle Pozzo river and the Parlati valley, is, along with Chiesa Nuova, one of the oldest districts in Positano.

Its original name was Ruparrata but this has only survived in local dialect. It tells us that the *Rupe* (the Rock) belonged to the old Parrata family that had settled there. Their name changed to Parlato over time, but there are area residents still bearing the older name. The upper part, which is right against the high rocky escarpment,

is known as *'ncoppa 'e cammere* (up to the rooms). This does not refer to houses but to the many natural caves. If we study its name more carefully, we realise its roots are Greek and so this takes us back in time, even though we are not sure how far. In Greek *kàmara* means both a vaulted room, and a cave. Thus, the dialect name should be taken as meaning "up to the caves" and was probably given by the Ba-silian monks when they arrived here from the East.

It is possible that these caves were used in the early Middle Ages as hermitages by monks or anchorites. More recently they became flock shelters, hay stores and, during the last World War, bomb-shelters for the inhabitants of the area, especially when Allied ships off Li Galli aimed their guns at the shipyards of Castellamare di Stabia.

OUR STOLEN CHILDHOOD - MEMORIES OF THE WAR DAYS

What did the war mean to us children? A wicked witch who did terrible things to everyone. We only knew about it because some of our uncles were fighting a war against an enemy.... but who was this invisible enemy who inspired so much fear and deprived us of our loved ones' affection? An ogre, straight from the pages of a horror book, who ate children and wanted to steal what little, and it was very little, we had. We had no toys, no shoes, no clothes and the ones we were wearing were practically in rags, handed down from older brothers not because they were out of fashion but because they had become too small. Our mothers taught us to pray in not very good Latin, asking for our loved ones to be protected and brought safely back home. We all did acts of mortification to ingratiate the powers to be and made promises and hoped to heaven that we, our beloved ones, and our town would be saved from grief and ruin.

On 2 February, 1943, the reality and terror of war touched us first-hand. Two merchant ships, the *Salemi* and *Valsavoia*, were sunk off Li Galli islands and it was only thanks to our local fishing vessels that the tragedy did not become a full-scale disaster.

Then, one night, we were woken up with a start by the sound of thunders, which shook the whole house. We children thought a huge storm was approaching. The thunderbolts did not signal the arrival of a storm but of enemy gunboats. Moored near Li Galli islands, their cannons were bombing - so we were told - the Castellamare shipyards. What did a cannon mean to us?

A dragon that could spew out fire a very long way.

A warship, what was a warship?

A giant sea-monster rising up from the depths to strike terror into people.

Wrapped in a blanket, shivering and bare-footed, our parents and older siblings held our hands and led us up a dark rickety staircase (was it the stairs or our legs that were shaking?) to a natural cave above the bedrooms.

In the pitch black, lit only by the flashes of gunfire, we tripped over and got silently up again. There was no time to lose. And you mustn't cry because, if you did, the fire-spewing dragon might hear you and find out where you were and gobble you up in an instant.

There were lots of our neighbours in the cave already and so, in the dim light of a shaded candle, we tried to find somewhere to sit, while other families continued to arrive with their toddlers and children who were all shivering and terrified by the cannon fire.

As far as we children were concerned, the dreaded invisible enemy we had only heard mentioned before, the ogre we feared yet we had escaped that far, seemed to be making his entrance in a much more violent and appalling way than we had imagined possible. The fact that the adults were scared stiff, and the palpable tension in the air, were contagious and made us little ones ever more afraid.

Huddled together under the blankets we wished we were invisible - or somewhere else. Our terror made us feel closer to each other.

In the absolute silence, broken only by the rumbling of the cannons, or the invocations to the Madonna of Positano that followed, we heard the feeble voice of one of our neighbours and a distant relative, Elvira Mazzacano, who exclaimed: "Let's recite a rosary!"

Everyone started praying; then, when day broke, the bombing stopped and a few men ventured out with my father to see what was happening and to make sure that the calm was real. They came back to reassure us and so, gradually, as the sun rose, we went back to our beloved homes, thinking about the time we had spent in the cave, which to us children had looked like ages.

How long had we been huddled up inside there? Only a few hours according to adult time-scales. Years, for us children.... Years had flashed by without us realizing it. The invisible enemy had come and, without us knowing, had robbed us of our innocence and our childhood.

The compact urban fabric and harmonious spontaneous architecture of Liparlati, with the houses built side to side and close together, simply developed over time, following the contours of the land, without overlooking the defensive needs. Its winding narrow streets, and long steep steps, which come out in wide open spaces like Piazzetta della Bellina, or smaller enclosed places like the churchyard of of S. Giacomo, as well as the houses grouped together not only for economic reasons, but for safety as well, all remind us of mediaeval hilltop towns, and make Liparlati hold a special place in our memories.

The only way to get to the sea from here was down the long steps of Via S. Sebastiano or Via Durece. The latter followed the course of the Valle Pozzo river and is a reminder of the 79AD "Plinian" eruption of Mt. Vesuvius, as the word *durece* refers to the mix of lapilli and ash that can still be seen in some rocky hollows and is somewhat less compact than Sorrento grey tuff.

The other route was down Via S. Sebastiano. Beside these steps, at the end of the first ramp down from Via G. Marconi, stood the chapel built by the Parlato family in honour of the saint. Only its memory survives.

Liparlati is also known as the Dead City, a name given to it after the unification of Italy when, at the end of the 19th century, the area suddenly emptied because of the number of able-bodied men who emigrated overseas with their dreams of fame and fortune.

Every two years, the young and very young work together to transform the district into a charming, living nativity scene.

Previous page:
Interior of S. Giacomo Church

Opposite:
Il campanile di S. Giacomo, by Raffaele Bella

Below:
Campanile detail and painting of the Last Supper

The Church of S. Giacomo

This is the district church and one of the oldest in Positano. It was founded in the 12th century, in honour of Santiago (S. Giacomo) de Compostela, by the Parrata family who had business interests in Spain. The church was the heart and soul of the mediaeval settlement of the district that developed around it.

Religious decorations found on the walls of some partially-ruined houses near the church leads us to believe that there was an adjoining monastery of which all trace has been lost.

Like most of these smaller churches, it had only one nave with a vaulted ceiling and four windows that lit the inside with its two altars.

The main altar is in inlaid marble and above it there is a framed picture of the Adorazione della Madonna col Bambino by S. Giacomo, S. Antonio – both "Spanish" saints – and other saints. During the S. Giacomo celebrations, the picture is replaced with a statue of the saint and the symbolic objects the pilgrims took with them to Compostela: a rope belt, a cloak and a shell. On the second altar on the right, which is made out of stone, there is a fine painting of The Last Supper with Jesus and the Apostles sitting at a round table. There is a cup in the foreground and it is probable that the artist's intention was to represent the Holy Grail, deemed to be the Last Supper chalice *or* the cup that was used to collect Christ's

255

blood on the cross. This chalice, it was believed, was housed in the sanctuary of Compostela.

Above the entrance is the *cantorìa* that can be accessed from the sacristy. In a niche facing the second altar, there is a collection of statues showing people from the world ethnical groups converted to Christianity.

S. Giacomo was the first church in Positano to be restored in the 18th century by Giovanni Cimmini and his sailors, after they escaped a shipwreck in 1707 by the miraculous intervention of S. Giacomo, as written in the much worn plaque inserted in the part-majolica floor. In the middle of the floor the symbols the pilgrims carried with them to Santiago de Compostela are shown: a rope belt with a knot in the middle, a cloak and a scallop shell[11].

A canvas in the sacristy symbolizes the Faith in the world with representatives from the different races. Outside, on either side of the door, there are two marble slabs with carvings of the apostles S.Giacomo and S. Giovanni (?), once shoulders of holy water fonts, bearing the names of donors and the year of apposition (1708 and 1709). The rather peculiar feature of the church, and therefore of the quarter, is the campanile with its unusual onion-shaped cupola and coloured tile decoration. Errico Talamo had this to say about it: "From the

257

sacristy an easy staircase leads to the top of the campanile, which is two floors and about seventy palms high. It is capped by a spire, and cannot be seen very clearly from a distance because of all the coloured decoration".

Giuseppe Vespoli added that "the Campanile is extremely unusual and all the artists have painted it against the background of the area because they find its colours and its simplicity incredibly artistic".

In the past the campanile was the central point of the area. Today, it has been restored, and to say that the restoration work was poor is an understatement. Its vibrant colours have been replaced by neutral shades that have stripped it of charm and beauty.

Between the church and Via G. Marconi there is a house called Casa Cimmino. It had to be the Cimmino family residence, the family that restored the Church of S. Giacomo.

The lost churches

Apart from the church of S. Nicola and the others mentioned above, there were several more churches and chapels scattered around the various districts of the town of Positano. The old abbey church of S. Vito, which was in the outer Sponda district, was suppressed and its title joined to that of today's church of the Assunta.

The others were the churches of SS. Trinità, S. Angelo de Torina, S. Maria del Grado on the old steep road up to Montepertuso, SS. Pietro and Andrea, near Piazza dei Mulini, S. Antonio del Monte, S. Paolo al Ponte, and the chapel of S. Antonio de lo Trasito *or* de la Gallinola, whose altar-frontal was taken to the church of S. Giovanni.

Along Via Mangialupini, as already mentioned, there is a beautiful 16th-century portal in grey tuff, with a cross sculpted on the gable. Maybe this portal is all that remains of the chapel of SS. Salvatore, which stood on this road. Further down the same road, on the garden wall of a villa, one can still see traces of 18th-century graffiti of sailing ships and other types of boats. Not to be overlooked are the chapels of S. Pietro de Pastiniello, and S. Giuliano, which were already in a bad state in 1550, and that of S. Sebastiano, down the steps of the same name which go from the Liparlati district down to the Marina. There is also the chapel of S. Croce, now part of a private house, on the corner of the road bearing the same name, which leads to the cemetery and up to Montepertuso, and the Maddalena chapel which used to stand where the Covo dei Saraceni hotel is now, as well as the SS. Annunziata chapel which used to stand in the namesake area, until it was demolished to make way for the Meta di Sorrento - Amalfi road.

Further proof of Positano's religious spirit can be noticed wandering up the old steps or along the paths leading to the tiny outlying hamlets, as there are along them lots of roadside shrines with majolica-tile paintings, nearly all of them dedicated to the Madonna or S. Giuseppe.

[1] On the subject, an eminent jurist had this to say: "It was a form of lease in Roman law but it was developed and clarified in mediaeval times when our countryside was in a sorry state. The *pastinato* contract was an attempt to make infertile and uncultivated land productive, because it forced the tenant to farm it". *Pastinare* actually meant breaking up the land and planting trees on it. This type of contract was very widespread during the Dukedom of Amalfi, and the actual document was called the *Charta incartationis*. The contract was for life and covered the chestnut and vine plantations. Any tenant taking land under it had to pay a sum of money after a certain number of years or else give over half of the produce. This is why an owner's inspector had to be present at the time of fruit picking.

[2] Fra' Nuvolo, formerly Giuseppe Donzelli, a Dominican monk from the Sanità convent in Naples, was one of the leading exponents of Neapolitan baroque.

[3] Vittorio Bracco, *Le urne romane della costa di Amalfi*, Salerno 1977.

[4] A "trabucco" was a war machine used to fire stones or shards at the enemy. The name is well suited to the presence of two watchtowers nearby and a fairly extensive system of forts in the area.

[5] This technique, which was a cheaper version of inlaid marble, consisted in replacing the pre-shaped coloured marble elements with a marble paste in the composition of ornamental designs on a flat surface. It was used from 16th century onwards in Emilia region and rapidly spread to Lombardia and Tuscany. In the South, it was popular in Campania and particularly in Irpinia.

[6] The Meleagros story is also depicted on a Roman sarcophagus housed in the Badia della SS. Trinità in Cava dei Tirreni.

[7] Vittorio Bracco, *Le urne…* cit.

[8] After the Council of Trent, new canons were adopted for the construction and renovation of churches. Pilasters were thus used instead of columns to give a greater impression of solidity – which was not purely spiritual. This was the period when many churches encased their existing columns inside pilasters.

[9] The icon at the Madonna del Granato Sanctuary, on the road to Capaccio Vecchio near Paestum, shows a Black Madonna celebrated on 15 August, as in Positano. The pomegranate was the symbol of *Hera Argiva*, the Sibarite goddess of plenty and the founder of Posidonia, which later became Paestum.

[10] The purpose was to let the bodies slowly drain their entrails wholesale through a hole in the seat – a most messy, distasteful, ghoulish and horrifying procedure luckily no longer in vogue – and thus yield a better mummification of the dead.

[11] Legend has it that, after Giacomo was beheaded by Herod Agrippa, the ship carrying his body was travelling along the Spanish coast when its sailors saw a knight on a white horse rise from the waves, covered in shells. These were taken as one of the symbols for pilgrims travelling to the Compostela sanctuary. S. Giacomo became the protector and personification of the fight against the Moors, the reason why he was nicknamed *Matamoros*. The pilgrimage to Compostela was considered as arduous as that to Jerusalem.

ITINERARIES
OF HISTORY

The Watchtowers

The long, dirty, undeclared war between Christianity and the Muslim world meant that, for nearly a thousand years, our town was exposed to attacks and raids from Saracen corsairs who, with the onset of the good season, would arrive in their agile boats, spreading terror and death. This continual state of alarm forced coastal towns to equip themselves with a new and valid system of defence against these "authentic sea-devils", as the Saracen pirates were called.

From the Sicilian Vespers war (1282-1302) onwards, pirate attacks intensified, thanks to tacit support from the Byzantine and Aragonese rulers who were in conflict with the Angevins.

King Carlo II, known as "the cripple" because of his physical handicap, sent out orders, on 9 March 1290, to defend the coastline, decreeing that watchtowers should be built along the coast which would warn of the approach of enemy ships by sending out smoke signals by day and fire signals by night so that the inhabitants could flee to safety or prepare to defend themselves[1].

The defence system that Southern Italy enacted was similar to that of other world powers.

267

For Positano, it entailed fortifying Li Galli islands, erecting wall segments (now disappeared) along the town's coastline and building three coastal watchtowers: Sponda, Trasino – later turned Trasita – and Fornillo or Jermano. Of these towers, witnesses to so many clashes and tragedies but now just mute stone guardians, only the Sponda retains some of the features of its original Angevin military architecture. Building on this tower started in 1277 and was completed in 1290. It stands on the rocky promontory to the east of Spiaggia Grande and can be admired in all its imposing beauty from the Sponda road junction or from the sea. It is cylindrical in shape, on a truncated conical base crowned by a jutting string-course of grey tuff. Access was at the level of the guards' station and was protected by a machicoulis protruding from the roof level. There was a ladder to get in, but it has been replaced with a stone bridge in more recent times. When artillery was introduced in the 16th century, the towers were restructured and equipped with loop-holes for the bronze cannons which were the pride of the Neapolitan arms factories.

On 6 September 1758, by order of the king Carlo di Borbone, the Lieutenant of the Artillery Corps, Gennaro Russo, took possession of the cannons from all three towers and transferred them abroad the *Madonna Assunta* tartan for the short voyage to Naples, where they were to be melt down in the local arsenal[2].

During the 1849 cholera epidemic, the Sponda tower was used as a burial chamber for the victims, and the Town Council paid 24 ducats on 20 July 1850 to Alessio Talamo, who had bought the tower from the Crown Property Office.

The top floor arms terrace is at present partly covered by a half-dome structure. But an old photograph, taken in the earliest years of the last century, shows that it had a still-intact flat roof. When the Pattison family, having purchased the tower in the 1920s, did reinforcement work on it, the roof had already partly collapsed, so it was changed to the way it looks now, and the tower became a home.

Following the Via Positanesi d'America which joins the two beaches, Spiaggia Grande and Fornillo, the cylindrical Trasita tower comes into view. It was originally called Trasino (meaning between two inlets or beaches) because its task was to keep guard over and protect both these beaches. Today's tower is a 1950s reconstruction of the old Angevin tower, which at that time was reduced to a few ruins.

A walk past the Trasino or Trasita tower, allows to see Positano's last coastal tower on the city's western side, standing on the rocky promontory at the end of Fornillo beach. This tower, unlike the other two,

had originally a square base overlain by a truncated-pyramid body, which means it was probably built in the 16th century as a result of the edict of the Viceroy Pedro de Toledo, reiterated by Viceroy Pedro Afán de Ribera. The tower was re-built in its current pentagonal shape by the Swiss writer and playwright Gilbert Clavel, who had bought it at the beginning of the 20th century, when it lay in ruins.

Apart from the external towers described, on a rocky spur near the Arienzo beach there was also a small fort built or re-built in 1809, during the decade of French domination in Naples (1806-1815), and armed with four 18cm-bore cannons. Its task was to deny the English flotilla, which had occupied Capri, access to water from the Porto river outlet, but only a semicircular base structure remains now. It is probable that a defence tower, of which all trace has been lost, already existed on the same site, also to prevent the Saracen ships from getting their water supplies. Some older maps point to the site as "Rienzo tower".

Within the town there were five more house-towers, which served as a refuge for the local population in case of attack. In the Chiesa Nuova district, between Via S. Giovanni and Via Marcello Montuori, there is the Seven Winds tower, with a truncated-pyramid base and tuff string course on top. Given its style and features, it can be assumed that it was built in the 16th century. As one continues along Via S. Giovanni, just before the little church of S. Giovanni, the walls of an inland tower come into view, they too being incorporated into newer buildings to the point that only sections of the pyramidal base and tuff string course can still be made out, implicating that it was probably built in the same epoch as the coastal ones. Further down, the remains of yet another tower can be seen, part of a private house now, with the top missing, which was linked to a more

extensive defence system. Again, only remnants of the tuff crown and the truncated conical base enable us to work out how big it was. The old name S. Giovanni, *or* Trabucco, referred to the fact that this tower was armed with a *trabucco*.

At the crossroad of Via S. Giovanni and Viale Pasitea, underneath the belvedere terrace, the Reginella tower can be seen, which was built at the same time and along similar lines as the other inland towers. It is well preserved and can be admired in all its splendour from the Sponda.

At the crossroad of Via dei Mulini and Via della Teglia, only the semicircular section of the garden wall of Hotel Palazzo Murat is sloped and crowned with corbels, whose outermost part is truncated. Was this the tower that used to defend the the abbey complex

before its church was expanded and built higher, thus obscuring the view of the sea?

Up the new road to Montepertuso the remains of the Giammarino tower rise on a rocky outcrop on the sea side. Its corbels, machicolis and the surrounding wall, which made it a true stronghold, are still visible. It was built by Giovanni Marino Mastrogiudice in the 17th century, as a deterrent for enemy attacks.

Halfway along the old Positano-Montepertuso footpath, in the Craro locality, a vague memory persists of the site where a fortified dwelling used to stand.

In listing the general defence system of Positano, we must mention again the tower on Li Galli main island, which was the first to be built, and the other defence structures on the Briganti island.

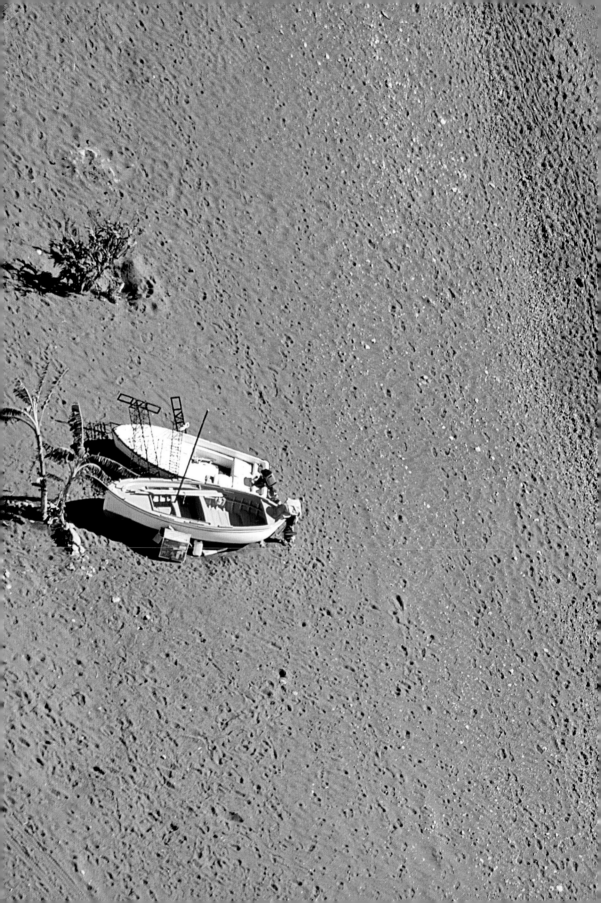

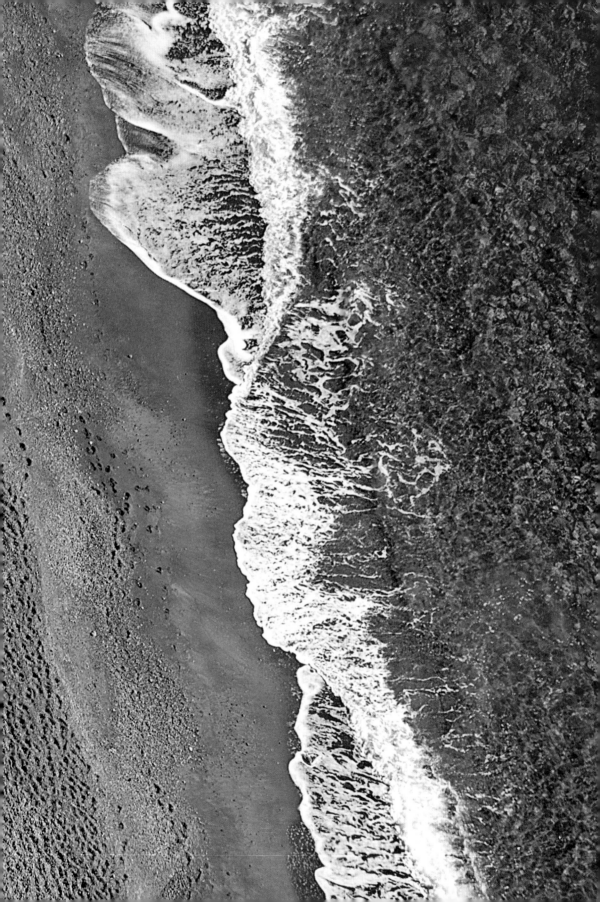

Eighteenth-century Villas and their Historical Gardens

The 18th century was a period of great economic prosperity for Positano, so much so that it earned the title "Gold Mountain". Some of the wealth, which was largely acquired through shipping trade, was used to renovate the churches and to build luxury residences along the lines of the villas that more famous architects were building at the time on the south-western slopes of Vesuvius.

The elegant villas built in Positano were a perfect combination of the new Baroque artistic trends and the building techniques used by local craftsmen. They are recognisable because of their structure, innovative technique, sloping tile-roofs, wonderful grey tuff portals with the family's coat of arms in the keystone, exterior stucco decoration, wrought iron fixtures and, in some cases, their still transpiring noble and opulent past. They provide important historical and cultural testimony and the fact that they are all so similar leads to believe that the same architect designed them all.

Palazzo Murat, now a top-of-the-line hotel, stands out in the crowd. It is a splendid 18th-century residence built on the remains of the old Benedictine Abbey. Even though the original family coat of arms has been erased from its tuff portal, its overall baroque appearance has been preserved intact, including the stucco decoration on the cornices of the balconies and the portly forged iron railings, typical of the period. In the middle of the large patio, which is what remains of the old abbey cloister, there are the remains

of an old cistern with its well-curb. In the corner a stairway, once made of compacted lapilli steps, connects the different floors. The building also has a large garden, originally an officinal herbs garden, which used to stretch beyond Via dei Mulini.

Today it is one of the most elegant and exclusive hotels in Positano. On its terrace, events are held that attract writers, poets, artists, and lovers of culture, literature and music from all over the world. We will only mention two of these events: the *Premio Sole, Arte e Cultura*, and the classical music concerts of the Associazione Positalta.

Over time, and as the hotel has grown, the garden has become more and more like a botanical garden because of the numerous exotic plants which have replaced the existing varieties, especially lemons and vines, which formed a pergola over part of Via dei Mulini[3], providing some shade to passers-by during the summer months.

Going back up to Piazza dei Mulini along Via C. Colombo one comes across Le Sirenuse hotel which opened in the 1950s when an 18th-century villa belonging to the Sersale family was renovated and extended. Although the hotel is only

Previous page:
La Sponda quarter

Opposite:
18th century villas along Via Cristoforo Colombo

Below:
Villa Orseola, formerly V

fifty years old, it has always been a major player in local history. Built around the original villa core, it has preserved some of its unusual features, and boasts spacious halls and terraces which look out over the majestic cupola of the Assunta Church, the sea and Li Galli islands. Le Sirenuse is counted among and most prestigious hotels in the world.

A bit further on, there are two other villas, which were the headquarters of an Allied command from 1943 to 1945. The first is partially annexed to the California hotel, and the second is a private house. In both cases, the original Baroque architecture has been preserved, including the room vaults with their splendid period frescoes. A bit further on there is the Gaetani dell'Aquila d'Aragona family villa, well known for its outstanding artistic features.

Continuing our ideal promenade, we get to Via S. Croce, commonly known in

the past as "the street of the long houses". There are along it four villas dating back to the same period, easy to spot because of their style and simple layout. They have a central staircase and the rooms are lined up on each side of it, on both the lower and upper floor, all of them looking out onto a terrace with a view. There is a side extension at each end of the terrace, supported by a portico on the ground floor. The resulting C-shaped construction pro-vided both a cover to the entrance, and guaranteed the villa a degree of safety and privacy.

The decision to build most of the villas on this south-facing slope was a winning choice on the part of our unknown architect because, apart from the wonderful view, these houses also get the sun in winter right until it sets beyond the sea.

Villa Orseola, formerly Villa Margherita, has preserved, better than any other, its

original stucco works, its doors and windows, and the panelling and the ceilings' decoration on the main floor. The villa garden has remained practically unchanged over time.

Two other smaller villas, a bit further on, just deserve mention, as does another one that was never finished, maybe because of the French occupation of the Kingdom of Naples.

Near the Chiesa Nuova crossroad stands Villa Stella Romana, owned by the Polish lady Emilia Szenwicz, who came to Posi-

tano just after the last World War. It is said that the late Pontiff Wojtyla also stayed in this villa when in his youth attended the seminar in Rome.

Until a few years ago, it kept a piano that had belonged to Chopin and that Léonide Massine played during rehearsals of the ballets he produced. For a time, it was also the seat of the Associazione Musicale Positalta.

Another villa, which was built much later, is currently annexed to the Buca di Bacco Hotel.

Opposite:
Keystone, villa Orseola entrance doorway

Below:
Positano Cemetery (upper centre) as seen from La Sponda

The Cemetery

"It is a sad man he who can visit a grave and does not feel moved, and looks coldly upon a marble tombstone as if he had no feelings. His soul does not know how to read the past, cares little for the present and even less about the future. By the same token, the man who feels his heart race at the sight of a monument and manages to see the links between the infinite nature of art and that of life, is a lucky one. He happily tries to find out the name and some details about the person who is buried there and breathes a sigh of compassion for those who deserve it, while uttering a curse for those who disgraced their name. A good lesson to learn for people who judge their own actions by what other people do and who expect the same post mortem rewards as their ancestors got. There is no better history book than tombs and epitaphs[4]".

The cemetery lies in the Santa Croce area, in the upper part of the town, on various levels, with the chapel in its centre. People of different religions are buried here without any distinction. The piety of Positano people has always respected and looked after the graves of foreigners who are buried there and have no family to care for them - like the Muslim writer Essad Bey, whose grave, facing Mecca, stands out because of its marble tombstone with

a turban on top, and the inscription of the first verse of the Holy Koran in Arabic script: "In the name of Allah, the most beneficent, the most merciful", followed by "Essad Bey 1905-1942", this last line also written in Italian. Not far away is the tomb of the Russian writer Michail Semenoff and his wife Valeria Teja, which looks out over the Arienzo mill. Teodor Massine - the father of Léonide – who died on Li Galli, is also here, and Ivan Zagoruiko, who had his favourite phrase inscribed on the grave: "How wonderful is the world of God". The daughter of writer Stefan Andres, Mechtild, who died of typhus in 1942 when she was still very young, Paula Bärenfänger, Zina Smolianova Hellestrom, Lidia Gisler Bachmann, Kurt and Anna Krämer, Marie Louise Philips, Eduardo Ghillausen, Hedwij Riedel Vivaldi, Lutka Gluckmann, Bruno Marquardt and many others, mostly refugees who chose to stay on in Positano after the war and end here their days.

It is a real pity that more recent funerary monuments have upset the quiet harmony of the past and the cemetery itself.

Previous page:
Vallone Porto and Arienzo beach
Below:
Moorish pavilion in Vallone Porto

The Vallone Porto Oasis

To the east of Positano, there is a deep rocky gorge which drops down several hundred metres, carved out by the Porto river which still runs at the bottom. Its waters used to feed the Arienzo mill behind the beach. The valley has its own microclimate and is a real haven of peace, a habitat of superior naturalistic interest, well worth to discover.

A path, leading up from the old forsaken road bridge on the Amalfi road, follows the river upstream through the hidden biological and natural varieties in the valley. Near the beginning there is an old lime oven, still in use until the 1950s, with two nearby water basins to prepare quick-lime: long dried up pieces of it can still be seen in one of them. A little bit further up is a kind of room, built into a natural cave, which was where the people who had the frightful task of keeping the furnace burning could rest and recover. On the right side of the bank is another basin, somewhat larger, which was originally the dyke for the Arienzo mill. When the mill ceased to function, even this one was turned to the production of quicklime.

Trekking up the valley along the narrow path, partly chiselled into the rocky walls where the limestone was quarried, one gets into an unspoilt, unusually humid and luxuriant environment. The river, with its succession of rapids and waterfalls, has

created a kind of Eden for some interesting flora and fauna. The woodland which lines the slopes is full of evergreens like ash, flowering ash, oak, bay oak, hornbeam, beech, alder, butcher's broom (which normally grow at much higher altitudes) and chestnut trees (here producing fruit at little more than fifty metres above sea level) as well as many other indigenous species.

In the spring, myrtle, juniper, rosemary, capers, strawberry trees, wild fennel, hawthorn, asphodel, clematis, mistletoe and numerous other aromatic and medicinal plants, like borage, thyme, rue, mallow, lemon balm, maidenhair, two different types of cyclamen, raspberry, ivy and many others, form a richly-scented blooming garden which attracts many butterflies, bees and other insects. On the rocky walls, thanks to the unusual microclimate, cling some special types of thermophile ferns, survivors from the Tertiary period, like *Pteris cretica* and *Pteris vittata,* and a very rare carnivorous plant, *Pingucula hirtiflora.* Wild orchids include *Ophrys fuciflora, Orchis italica, Neottia nidus-avis* and various others.

The extremely rare *Salamandrina terdigitata* or *perspicillata,*which is endemic in Italy, breeds in the ponds.

The birds of prey in the valley include the peregrine falcon, sparrow hawk, kestrel and buzzard. The Swabian Emperor Federico II, who loved falconry, had these birds trapped within the canyon, which is still a breeding place for them today.

Nocturnal birds of prey include owls, barn owls and tawny owls. Seven types of bats are representative of nocturnal mammals. In springtime it is not uncommon to see hoopoes, kingfishers, woodcocks and other types of migratory birds. Mammals include foxes, water voles, hedgehogs, moles, badgers and many more[5].

The furthest and deepest part of the gorge holds a surprise: a garden with a Moorish pavilion and a fountain cut out of the wall supporting the upper terrace, complete with swirls and cornices, made out of black and white stone, which is similar to the decoration on a fountain at Villa Campolieto in Herculaneum. The similarity of style leads to think that the garden and fountain were built in the 18th century, when the valley was a dependency of the villa called *Il Palazzo del Generale,* now in ruins on the ridge looking towards Positano.

Following the *Sentiero* (path) *del Generale* it was possible get to this garden from the villa, on horseback even, and enjoy a bit of cool during the torrid summers. Before the Meta-Amalfi road was built, this was the only way to get to the Vallone Porto. The garden, the pavilion and the fountain with its geometric decoration, all appear to indicate that the workmanship employed was not local but from North Africa: probably part of the group of Moorish prisoners who built the Royal Palace in Caserta and the steps up to Montepertuso and S. Maria del Castello, also built this delightful, restful garden.

It was here that in the last century the Swiss biologist Octo Bauer, to the

nervousness of the natives, carried out his marine biology experiments and research into amphibians.

The valley, which is still a natural Eden, was a hermitage and home to the artists Valy Myers and Rudy Rappold, who both died only a few years ago. They defended it from "developers" and speculators from the day they arrived in 1958 until the day they died. The versatile artist Gianni Menichetti has become their spiritual heir and self-appointed custodian, and he loves to paint the flora and fauna between writing a poem or a short story.

Back to the Amalfi road and below it, the dyke and pressure tower of the Arienzo mill, down near the beach, come into sight.

NOTES

[1] In an edict sent out during the Aragonese period we read: "...*If you discover that enemy ships are approaching, or if you suspect as much because of this structure, type or way they are sailing, you should immediately warn people by firing the mortar or cannon once, followed by a smoke signal if it is daytime, or a fire signal at night, from the top of the tower. If you cannot see enemy vessels, or anything that might be suspected as such out at sea, but you see smoke or fire signals being sent out from the towers within sight of your own, you should respond with similar smoke or fire signals from the top of the tower*".

[2] The royal order came with this notice, delivered in Positano to city officers on 6 September 1758: "... *we would like to inform you that since the King has decreed that the bronze cannons in your towers be dispatched by sea, we are sending you this letter so that you can organise immediately for the cannons to be lowered from the towers and taken down to the beach. There, they will be loaded onto the ships by D. Gennaro Rossi, Head of Ar-tillery Corps, who is in charge of operations. You should get a receipt from him detailing the expenses you incurred. Anyone failing to obey these instructions will be fined one hundred ducats. You should respond to this letter (...) with a written report and it is your responsibility to make sure we receive it. For your information, you don't need to worry if any of the cannons get broken because they are going to be melt down*".

The relevant certificate states that the following pieces of artillery were lifted from Positano towers: "*Sponda Tower, bronze cannons, two. Trasita Tower, bronze cannons, one. Germano Tower, bronze cannons, two. Cannon balls, 28*".

[3] During the 1920s the Podestà (Mayor) asked Mr. Alfonso Cinque, owner of the building, to cover Via dei Mulini with a pergola, thus making it the most charming and loved street in the town

[4] Matteo Camera, *cit.* vol. I, p. 666.

[5] For more information on the Vallone Porto we recommend Gianni Menichetti's book *Il Porto, storia di un canyon selvaggio*, Maiori 2003.

THE
THREE
HAMLETS
OF POSITANO

Montepertuso

Situated at some 350 m. above sea level, Montepertuso (pierced mountain) appears with its splendid arch, the most spectacular natural feature of Monte Gambera, standing above the village.

The area itself is made up of two tiny separate hamlets, Cappella to the west and Pestella (little Paestum) to the east, which takes its name from the Paestum refugees who settled here after they fled from the final Saracen raid of 24 June 916. Cappella has a small piazza, at the end of which stands a devotional pillar similar to others often found in the Lattari Mountains settlements.

Its origins are lost in the mists of time. Tradition has it that in 553, a band of Ostrogoths took shelter here from certain death after their last king Teia was defeated by the Byzantine general Narses on the Sarno river plain.

Popular stories aside, we are inclined to think that this is one of the many farming villages which took to the hills as a safeguard measure against Saracen marauders from the 7th- 8th- century onwards.

Early records refer to a grange administered by the Positano abbey, which owned the whole land.

THE LEGEND OF THE GOTHS

I am the last survivor of the Ostrogoth army led by king Teia and defeated by the Byzantine general Narses on the plain beyond the hills.

I was part of that fine people, the Eastern Goths, who inhabited the misty Nordic lands; greedy for conquest we came down to the fertile lands of the Romans, reaching the southern sea.

More than once we fought the Byzantine army, who forced us northwards.

We were camped on a plain near Nuceria and Pompeii between the river Sarno and a smoking mountain called Vesuvius, when, at first light, we were attacked by the Byzantine army, who wrought a terrible Greek fire upon us which set all ablaze and which water could not extinguish.

Though taken by surprise we defended ourselves bravely. Our king, Teia, rode along our lines encouraging the faint-hearted. The battle swung one way and another and lasted till sunset. Our king, continued to fight incessantly and give heart, until a javelin struck his chest and killed him.

His death stunned us. Our army began to lose ground and disband.

I and other companions in charge of the flank at the foot of the Lattari Mountains, taking advantage of the darkness as the Greeks ravaged our rich encampment, climbed the wooded hills that hid us from sight of the enemy. In the middle of the night, exhausted and starving we came across a clearing, where we rested briefly for fear that we might be reached by the Byzantines, notorious for their ferocity towards barbarian prisoners.

At first light we continued our flight to get as far away as we could from our enemies.

We wandered through the mountains in search of a sign that might give us courage.

One morning we were drawn towards a cliff with a huge hole through which the rays of the sun shone. It was a good omen so we decided to halt and take rest and refreshment with the cheese and milk that some shepherds, taking pity on us, had kindly offered.

It was in our hearts to return to our lands but an invisible force, of which we were unaware, held us there.

Time passed and we, nomads, learned to love these mountains and the land we farmed. Our tents became huts and our huts would become dwellings.

At the foot of this pierced mountain, which had beckoned us during our wandering, we decided to settle and gradually contributed to expand a tiny village called Montepertuso – like the mountain it clung to.

In the past its economy was mainly based on farming, as shown by the many terracings around it. Montepertuso was famous for its fine dairy products and meat, not to mention the excellent quality of olive oil, as, up until a few years ago, the many oil mills equipped with screw presses, known as "*genovesi*" bear testimony.

Its inhabitants, like those of Nocella, lived in perfect harmony with nature.

Today, this village is easily reached by a new motor road but it was not long ago that only two steep paths reached the village from Positano. The first from Via Liparlati, up the Tese di S. Giuseppe, attained Montepertuso in Piazza Cappella, where other footpaths lead to the higher reaches of the Lattari Mountains; the second, older path, from Via Santa Croce reached Pestella.

It is advisable to walk these nature paths over the ridge to admire the breathtaking views and the stunning natural landscape. The farmlands and terracings, built up with limestone boulders and covered by olive groves, vines and lemon trees, are particularly fascinating. This healthy walk through woods and gardens is worth every bit of the effort it requires.

On the plateau overlooking the village stands the church of the Madonna delle Grazie rising from a large courtyard. Its simple, plain architecture with semicircular apse and side chapels brings to mind similar examples of Renaissance architecture, though various layers of restoration work over the years, as so often happens, have caused it to lose its original shape.

THE LEGEND OF THE MADONNA OF MONTEPERTUSO

On a freezing cold dawn the Madonna and her friends headed barefoot, as they did each morning, to fill their pitchers at the old fountain, around a bend along the rough path suddenly appeared the devil, who blocked their way.

Startled, Mary's friends fell back and began to tremble and weep, while Mary, completely unconcerned by this presence from hell, stood still.

I am Beelzebub! – boomed the devil – the mightiest master of the abyss. He who can do all and who is served by hordes of devils a thousand times more numerous than hosts of angels. To show that I speak the truth I shall reveal my power so that you, convinced of my might, may worship me as your one and only lord. Do you see that mountain behind? With my hands, in an instant, I shall open it up so that you may return home more easily.

This said, he disappeared.

Mary encouraged her friends, still trembling, and said: Do not be afraid! As long as you stay with me you will have nothing to fear.

After a while the noise of stones crashing below, inhuman screams, mixed with unrepeatable blasphemies and curses, echoed down the valley. It was obvious that the rock was harder and the task more demanding than the devil had envisaged.

Mary and her friends went to the spring, filled their pitchers with fresh water and began their journey home.

At the foot of the hills the devil continued to curse and swear because, despite his efforts and blows against the hard rock, he could not manage to progress beyond a tiny dent in opening up the mountain which continued, undismayed, to resist his blows.

Mary observed with great pity his useless fatigue and vain efforts which revealed not his might, but his incapacity and impotence.

Do not tire yourself further – she said – your might is nothing compared to the power of God. Go back to your kingdom of darkness where my one and true God banished you, but first, so that you might not tempt me, nor those under my protection, watch how with one light touch of my hand, guided from on high, I shall succeed, in an instant, where you have failed, despite your efforts and infernal might directed towards evil.

Then she came close to the mountain and stroking it with her hand, cried: In the name of God, open up!

The solid rock opened and a blinding ray from the rising sun flooded her splendid figure in divine light.

The devil, scorned and defeated, hurled himself down the mountain, gone forever. As he fled from this blessed place he fell on the bare rock of the path where, at the first light of day, his encounter with Mary had occurred, leaving a giant footprint and the imprint of his tail, which can still be seen today.

From that day on, to record this prestigious event, the village was called Montepertuso in honour of the Madonna, and to her, elected Queen and Protector, a temple at the top of the village was dedicated.

Previous page:
Montepertuso church interior

Opposite:
Dedication stone of the church

Below:
Inscribed tiles salvaged from the old floor

This church must have been founded shortly after the Chiesa Madre of Positano. A stone, previously affixed to the campanile and now placed against the wall at the entrance to the right-hand nave, records in Latin: "This temple to the Holiest Maria delle Grazie di Montepertuso, long since collapsed, was rebuilt by a generous banker so that the ashes of his ancestors buried here would no longer be exposed to the elements, and he repaired the roof of the campanile too. Following the example of his father, Giacomo completed the work and equipped it throughout in 1531".

A few inscribed majolica tiles from subsequent restoration in the 18th century, when the church took on its present aspect, are housed in the sacristy.

The pseudo-Baroque interior has three naves, separated by arches. Two small holy water stoups stand to the sides of the entrance, devotional gifts of the Perrella family. Above the altar in a niche is a painting which has been impossible to date accurately but which represents the *Visita della Madonna a Santa Elisabetta*. To the sides of the altar are recent frescoes of saints Peter and Paul and on the right-hand wall a marble inscribed in Latin "Holy Oil of the Sick" is enclosed in a niche.

Entering from the right-hand nave, below the aforementioned 16th-century dedication stone is a walled-in funerary stone reciting in Latin (see photo on p. 311): *"To the Gods of the Underworld we trust the soul of Lucius, son of Vitulinus, who lived*

happy for thirty years, most piously, with his well-deserving consort".

To the right of the first arch is a painting of S. Giovannino; at the second arch dividing the naves stands an altar in inlaid marble with a 1819 devotional inscription. Above the altar a painting with S. Anna, S. Gioacchino and an adolescent Madonna represents the Education of the Virgin. The chapel to the right of the altar, which houses the precious statue of the Madonna delle Grazie, bears a 1826 devotional inscription. On the wall of the left nave, near the first arch, is a valuable reliquary of the Cross, embroidered with beads. The second altar

in the left-hand nave was bequeathed in 1827. The other two altars, similar in size, bear no inscription. Above the entrance is the *cantorìa* with organ. The main nave ceiling is barrel-vaulted with eight lunettes and as many windows. In the upper part of the apse is a round skylight which, when struck by sunrays, creates a very special atmosphere.

The sacristy is also a sort of small museum of sacred art, brought together by don Andrea Imperati. It houses several precious ornaments used in the past as well as some marble bas-reliefs: a Madonna with Child placed above a holy

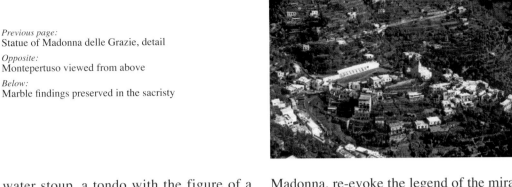

water stoup, a tondo with the figure of a saint, a funeral urn with cherub, a marble bas-relief of S. Antonio da Padova and other marble and sacred objects, almost all of them recovered from the former private chapel of S. Gennaro, which stood in a villa in Liparlati.

To the right of the church stands the campanile with its characteristic irregular octagonal cusp. From the splendid terraced churchyard, the eye can space from the isles of Li Galli and the Faraglioni of Capri to an encompassing view of the wild green beauty of the Monti Lattari.

On July 2, feast of S. Maria delle Grazie, the inhabitants, deeply devoted to the Madonna, re-evoke the legend of the miracle of the pierced mountain, performed with a simple touch of the hand by the Madonna, humiliating in this way the devil who was attempting, in vain, to perform the that same prodigy. A nearby cave (*La grotta del diavolo*) is indicated as the result of the devil's failed, clumsy attempt. Some hollows in the rock, lower down, eroded by streams, are said to be the footprints and tail imprint of the devil.

This natural area can only be reached on foot from Via Campola, which starts from piazzetta Cappella, and from the steps leading into Via Dragone, at the beginning of the village.

Previous page:
Montepertuso

Opposite:
Ancient print of Madonna delle Grazie

Below:
Statue of the Madonna and embroidered canvas of the
Madonna delle Grazie (1815)

Montepertuso today, though irreparably scarred by the unheeding new road to Nocella, an unsightly sports field and buildings constructed without taking into account traditional techniques and the size and features of the area in question, does maintain, almost unchanged, a network of old alleyways and lanes leading to hamlets nearby. Strolling down these winding streets and steps it is still possible to admire the harmonious examples of its simple, spontaneous architecture and enjoy the beauty of its landscapes, its vistas and an almost unreal peace.

Nocella

Perched on a hill between land and sea, keeping an eye on a wide stretch of sea for Saracen pirates, Nocella is situated at around 450 m. above sea level between Vallone Porto and Vallone Capriglione and is towered over by Monte S. Croce. Nocella was founded by Paestum inhabitants fleeing from Saracen hordes in 916.

Careless scholars attributed its name to the hazelnut plant fruit, *nocciola*, changing the ancient village of Nocella into Nocelle.

A more accurate study of its etymology renders justice to its historical, not botanical origins. Nocella actually derives from the Greek *neos oicos* through the Latin *nova cella* (new dwelling or new chapel), which was the name given by refugees from Paestum to their new home.

Up until a few years ago, a delightful natural pathway connected it to Montepertuso and flights of steep steps to Positano. Nocella is now linked to these two areas by the Montepertuso road and is easy to reach.

For those who enjoy wandering into a peaceful environment, the old pathway from Montepertuso to Nocella is perfect: it follows a winding route across the ridge, from a rough, wild landscape to the green woods of Mediterranean maquis and to panoramic viewpoints which offer a view of the whole coastal belt and the deep and spectacular gorge of Vallone Porto, with its steep cliffs eroded by the river and reddened by the sunrays.

THE LEGEND OF NOCELLA

And so we have arrived from the lands on the other side of the gulf of Poseidon, from the ancient city of Paestum.

We had just learned that the Saracens, based at the mouth of the river Garigliano, had been defeated by a Christian fleet and that the rest of their miserable crew had set sail for Africa.

We got word, perhaps purposely put about, that the Saracens in Agropoli, always the object of our surveillance, also were on their way to Africa.

That night was a happy one because our feared enemy was finally about to leave our lands. We took to our beds with the thought of a new beginning.

How wrong we were!

We dismantled the city walls in the belief that the treacherous Saracens were going away.

But in that holiest night of S. Giovanni they landed on our shores, thirsty for Christian blood and hungry to take revenge for the defeat they had suffered.

Their trumpets sounded the anthem of war and under cover of darkness they entered our places, plundering our churches and looting our homes, impetuously leading on their young slaves, thrusting their swords in the hearts of the fearless trying in vain to defend themselves from this insane greed.

On hearing news of the size of our enemy and living far from the shore, frightened and horrified we sought escape from their blood lust and certain death, fleeing up the mountains behind, imploring and entreating through our tears: God, save us and our children who have done no wrong! Punish the arrogance of your enemies who have shown no respect for your sacred altars!

We reached a place called Capo d'Acqua and from up there, at the first light of day, we saw the cursed Saracen galleys leaving the shores and the smoking ruins of our dwellings, loaded with their spoils and prisoners to be sold as slaves in distant lands.

Shocked by the huge tragedy, for the loss of so many persons dear to us and all our worldly goods, we decided, albeit reluctantly, to abandon our home and set out for more secure terrain.

What safer and more comfortable place than ours might we now seek?

Who could dare give exile to a horde of fugitives?

Many ideas came to mind.

Some wanted to stay on the mountains behind Capo d'Acqua and steadily built up a town, known today as Capaccio. Reluctantly we decided to leave our land promising in our hearts to return, as we had no wish to sever the ties of family and friends.

With the goodwill of rescuers and lucky winds we came to these shores to ask for asylum and help from the Basilian friars, who had founded an abbey to the martyr S. Vito. - We are refugees from Paestum! We were attacked by the Saracens who slaughtered our loved ones and took away our property.

We told of the sad end of our hometown and continued: - In the name of God, help us.

The friars and the people who had come running to see us in our dreadful state replied: - You are welcome, and though our land is not so fertile, we will make sure it is sufficient for you and for us.

They entrusted us with land to till and farm east of Montepertuso, which we named Pestella, little Paestum, so as not to forget our lost home, and also further up, at the foot of a mountain called S. Croce. This place, with its wide view across the sea, allowed us to see on a fine day our distant shore, our lost home, and to keep our emotional ties alive, but as it was easy to defend, it placed us in safety against any raids by the wicked Saracens, whose boats we could spot early and avoid incurring a tragedy the like of which we had already experienced.

We began to love this land and after harvesting the first fruit of our labours we built a chapel and around it the first dwellings. We called our new home Nova Cella.

Halfway down its course, Vallone Porto is spanned with a single arch by a mediaeval bridge. It is the oldest bridge in the area and along the whole Amalfi Coast.

After centuries of honourable service, a total and unforgivable lack of historical and environmental sensibility had it overshadowed by a reinforced concrete bridge, which forms part of the new road.

Ancient fear of ravines, believed to be inhabited by devils or damned souls gave rise to one of the many legends embellishing our history. The tale goes that the resident devil of the ravine did not wish the inhabitants of Montepertuso and Nocella to build a bridge, and therefore at night-time he dismantled the work carried out during daylight.

After many vain attempts the inhabitants of the two villages were forced to make a pact with the devil who, in exchange for allowing the bridge to be built, would have the right to the soul of the first living being to cross the bridge.

On that fated day the people of Montepertuso arrived accompanied by ravenous hounds and from Nocella with a black cat tied up in a sack. Those with the cat

positioned themselves at one end of the bridge, those with the dogs at the other end, then the dogs and the cat were freed. On seeing the cat, the dogs ran headlong across the bridge while the cat ran for shelter in the woods, and so the devil had to make do with the soul of the fastest dog in the crowd. In all honesty it has to be said that the devil kept his word as the bridge is still standing after over a thousand years!

The ancient village, which winds its way along a narrow lane leading to a church a little downhill, begins with a natural archway, less impressive than that of Montepertuso, and numerous terracings that cut the slope down toward the sea.

Like Montepertuso, the local population gave itself to agriculture and pasture. Up until a few years ago it was famous for its high quality cheese, meat and farm produce and has preserved its original character as a rural village with typical spontaneous architecture and country charm.

It is still possible here to discover the age-old relationship between man and nature. Most of its detached or terraced farmhouses, which wind along the only pedestrian lane in the village, have a steeper pyramidal hip roof than in Positano to stop snow from piling up in the winter months.

The church, built in 1834 by Giuseppe Casola and the village inhabitants to replace the older church, now the cemetery chapel, is dedicated to the Madonna del Carmelo.

It has just one nave with lowered barrel-vaulted ceiling and apse with a simple altar, above which a 17th century painting of the Deposizione di Cristo is housed in a niche. Here too the two rooms of the sacristy make up a small museum of ethnography and religious art, put together, as in Montepertuso, by don Andrea Imperati. The most valuable item is a funeral urn in white marble, encased in the wall and used in the past as a baptismal font.

It is the same size as the two urns at Positano. On the front side, the only one visible, the following inscription in Latin appears, supported by small pillars: "*To the gods of the underworld* [the soul is

entrusted] *of Marcia Iusta, daughter of Lucius* [Marcius Iustus]. *Iustus, her fater* [wrote this inscription]". Not all scholars interested in our history and monuments mention this funerary urn, but just that of the Chiesa Nuova and the church of S. Giovanni.

In the 1960s, the church was plundered and many precious objects were stolen, including a silver ball with brass foot, a silver pyx and a silver censer with boat.

The large church courtyard is, like that of Montepertuso, a viewing terrace, from which the eye can span a wide landscape, unique in the world, which takes in the Bay of Salerno from Punta Licosa to Capri. Behind, stand the rugged, rocky backdrop of the Monti Lattari range, from its highest peak to the plateau of S. Maria del Castello, Monte Comune and, further down, Montepertuso and Positano with its coastline dotted with watchtowers and beaches. Unfortunately, the unsightly iron posts and cables of the electricity grid have irreparably scarred a landscape of rare beauty and harmony.

Among the folk tales recounted in this place, there is that the famous brigand *Scorticaciuccio* (donkey-skinner), who overran the Lattari after the Kingdom of Naples was annexed to Italy.

He made a certain signor Casola a gift of a life-size tray with hen and a dozen chicks, in solid gold, in exchange for his help and hospitality. Another version it that Joachim Murat, in flight towards Calabria, passed by with a convoy of more

335

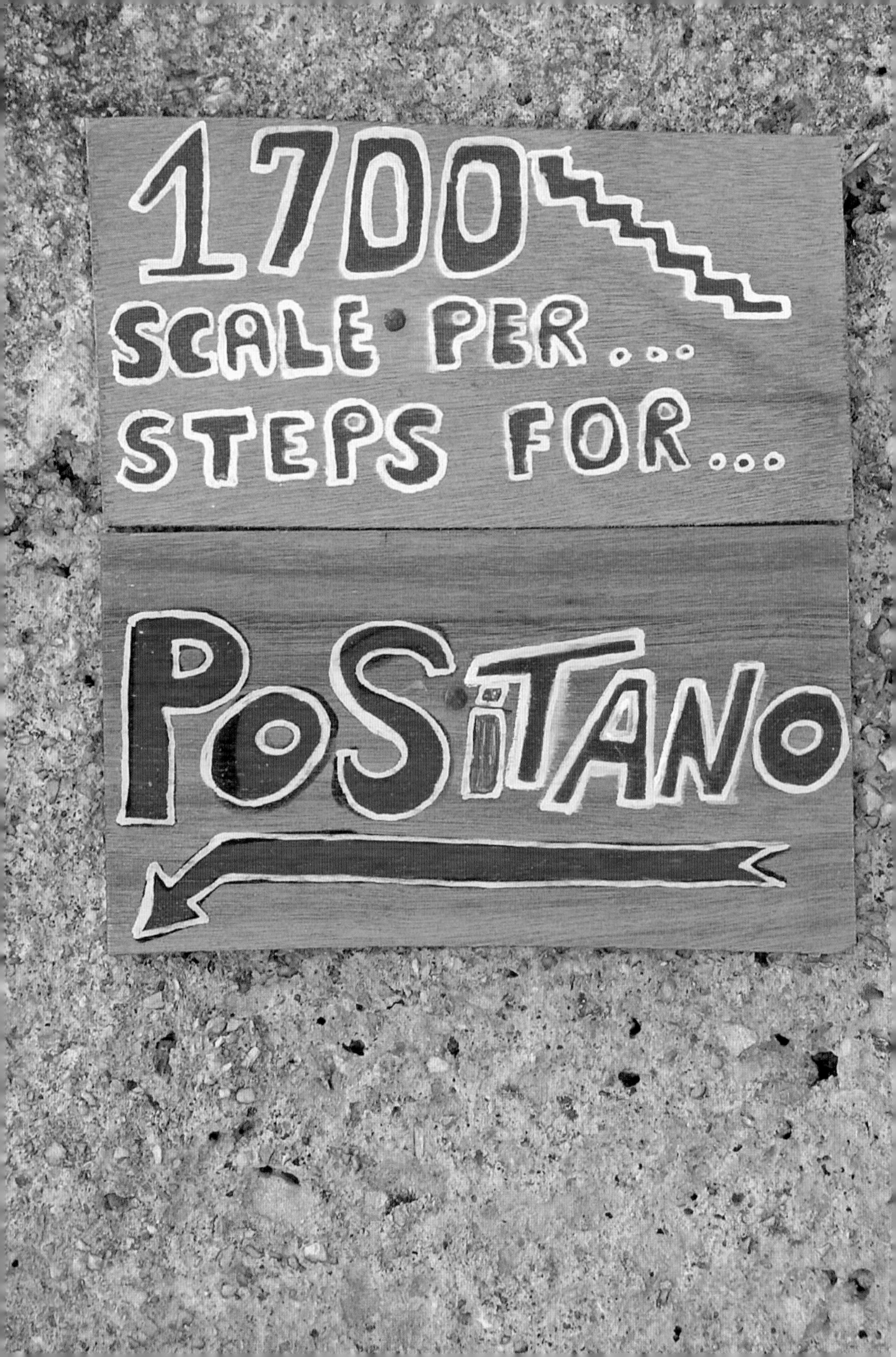
1700
SCALE PER...
STEPS FOR...
POSITANO

Previous page:
Signpost showing route

Below:
Organ, floor detail and churchyard of Madonna del Carmelo
Church

than a thousand mules and left this valuable object in exchange for the help and hospitality he received.

Following the unification of Italy many would leave for the shores across the ocean.

Laurito

At some two kilometres from Positano, towards Amalfi, stands Laurito, one of the oldest villages of Positano and perhaps of the whole Amalfi Coast. Some of those who fled from Paestum also found refuge there. In the past, remains of ancient walls were unearthed at Laurito, along with a considerable amount of Greek coins and clay vases.

In 991 the Saracen pirate Boalim, after raiding the other towns and villages of the Amalfi Coast, attempted to plunder Laurito as well: "And so the inhabitants of Laurito squared up to them shouting and hurling stones. The infidels were startled and retreated, took to their boats and decided to carry on by sea", as reported by A. Mattiello (*cit.*).

In the early 19th century a landslide brought to light the remains of a wall constructed in reticulate stonework along with mosaics which adorned an artistic fountain, "destroyed by the brave hand of the ignorant", as Matteo Camera sagaciously noted in his time.

Beneath the first church dedicated to S. Pietro, which was located near the beach where the Albergo delle Sirene stands

today, the fisherman Diodato Laino discovered a small gold statue of a mythological divinity, which he sold for three hundred ducats in 1823.

The name Laurito is said to derive from the many laurel plants that grow wild here. In reality the name is not unique to this area (among the estates spread across the land the abbey of Positano owned property in another Laurito in the Cilento area) and actually derives from *laura*, a form of community somewhere between the coenobium and the hermitage.

The village was densely populated in the past, as the many ruins often unearthed show. The ruins themselves served as retaining walls for the various terracings constructed after a massive landslide destroyed a large part of the village. Most of the inhabitants earned their livelihood by alternating fishing and farming. The chapel, dedicated to the apostle Peter and built by Filippo Talamo in the upper part of the village following the collapse of the previous chapel closer to the beach, is rectangular in plan with a single nave and vaulted ceiling and has no particular architectural merit.

Thanks to its privileged panoramic position, which takes in the whole arc of the

Sorrento Peninsula and Capri, and to the far-sightedness of the Positano businessman Carlo Cinque, Laurito is now home to one of the most famous hotels in the world: Albergo San Pietro, which stands on the rocky ridge below the chapel.

NATURAL
FEATURES

Previous page:
Grotta del Cadavere and (to the left) solarium of Albergo
S. Pietro
Below:
Grotta La Porta

The caves

The morphology of the Lattari limestone massif is characterised by karst features caused by surface and underground water action. A large number of caves have given shelter to man and animals alike over thousands of years. Almost none have been fully mapped or explored, though they could easily fit into nature trails, which could realize their attraction potential and provide them proper protection. Much has been said on La Porta cave, where over three hundred items, dating back to the Paleolithic, were unearthed. Little now remains of this cave due to frequent collapses over the course of centuries as well as the construction of a new road.

Just beyond the cemetery, on private property, lies the Grotta di Mirabella. Three metres above its floor a narrow tunnel leads to the first chamber, with some fine, almost transparent stalactites and stalagmites and other natural features. The cave narrows as it enters the earth's bowels with hollows and other small unremarkable spaces. The story goes that the brigand Mirabella, who lived astride the 18th and 19th centuries and gave his name to the cave, had stashed a huge treasure of gold, silver, precious stones and twelve sacks of gold coins there, the fruits of robbery and extortion. Three intrepid youngsters from Positano attempted to seize the treasure with the help of an old hag from Fornillo, to whom they promised half the spoils. A violent death awaited them and since then no one has ever tried to get their hands on the fabulous treasure hidden among the hollows of the cave.

The Grotta di Capriglione lies above Laurito and is difficult to access. It is made

up of a large cavity and a very deep tunnel, at the end of which is a tiny hollow carved out by dribbling water. For centuries the cave was a refuge for shepherds and their flocks.

The Grotta del Generale is situated along the path which used to lead to Vallone Porto, where caves abound. Another shallow cave at high altitude, which is visible from Positano, is in a place called Fiossa. This is the Grotta di Mezzogiorno or delle Soppressate (a kind of sausage), so called either because as of midday sharp it lies in total shade, or because its numerous stalactites convey the plebeian idea of a delicatessen shop with a plethora of salami hanging from the ceiling. Palaeolithic finds in the 1950s were also made here.

Along the Tese di S. Giuseppe, which lead to S. Maria del Castello, thirty metres up a sheer cliff, partially closed by a small wall blending into the surrounding rocks, is another cave, now inaccessible, said to be very deep and to have a second entrance or exit in Vallone Capo d'Acqua, utilised by brigands as an escape route. In realty the cave is tiny and the arquebusier in the clos-

ing wall suggests that it was either a look-out or an anti-smuggling post.

The caves above Liparlati quarter have already been discussed.

Other caves, many inaccessible or yet to be detected, are widespread amongst the Monti Lattari.

But inland caves are not the only ones this area can boast. Along the craggy coastal cliffs are many more caves that are less well-known than other famous marine caves. One of these, extending some ten metres from the entrance, lies below the Fornillo tower. Inside is a tiny stretch of sand and some steps cut into the rock by Gilbert Clavel, leading to the tower. Another one, not easily accessible, with cobalt blue waters, is the Grotta del Cadavere (corpse), situated beneath the San Pietro Hotel in Laurito. It gets its name from the waxy colour of the skin taken by those who dive in. Some other steps carved into the rock lead to a farmhouse further up.

Near the Laurito beach, on the side of Vettica di Praiano, there is a cave with fresh-water pool. In the past fishermen would draw water here before setting out on their night-time fishing expeditions.

Mother and Child

In the sea just off the Fornillo tower there were two rocks named *Mamma e Figlio* because of their respective size. A ceramic effigy of the Madonna di Positano was placed on the larger of the two and the night fisherman would light a candle there and pray for protection and a plentiful catch.

On August 15, Feast of the Assumption, a procession of fishing boats and private launches used to carry a statue of the Madonna there.

On February 23, 1943 one of the stray torpedoes launched by the British submarine *Safari*, which sank two Italian merchant ships en route to Africa, the *Valsavoia* and *Salemi*, demolished a large part of the rock known as *Mamma*. Popular belief took it as a sign of love and sacrifice by the mother for her child. A few years later, a violent storm knocked down the *Figlio* all the same.

The ceramic effigy of the Madonna, still intact, is visible a few metres below the surface.

CULTURE
AND
FOLKLORE

Previous page:
Gioacchino Romano

Opposite:
Vintage postcard of the "Saracen landings" acted play

Below:
Players re-enacting the Saracen landings (photo from *Positano è*)

Folk traditions have all but disappeared, though there were many events in the past, which recalled the sad and joyful moments of life in the area.

The most famous of these, in terms of popularity beyond the confines of the local area, was the "Landing of the Saracens", which evoked the legend of the transient plundering of the painting of the Madonna by the Saracens on the evening of August 14 of an unspecified year.

To make the most of this event, youngsters of Positano would divide themselves up equally between Christians and Saracens to re-enact the sea and land battle to defend the town from attack. After slaughtering the defence detail, the Saracen pirates would plunder and set fire to the church, built on the quay out of wood and straw, only after they had removed the precious painting. As soon as they were off the shore a voice would cry *posa posa* (lay me down) to persuade them to come back and return the miraculous image.

The re-enaction took place for the last time in 1954.

Worth mentioning are the *Festa del Pesce* in late summer, the *Sagra della Zeppola* - a traditional Christmas treat eaten to welcome the new year – and the Nativity live scene.

Religious feasts

Positano devotes a very particular celebration to its Madonna dell'Assunta, derived from history and myth. August 15 has always been the paramount local feast. After the procession had solemnly passed along the seashore, people would collect pebbles with holes in them to keep as a lucky charm or amulet because they were believed to have been touched by the Madonna as she passed. The strictly religious festival is now brought to a close with a fireworks display at sea and attracts thousands of people and hundreds of boats from the Amalfi Coast and the Sorrento Peninsula.

S. Vito, protector saint of the town, is celebrated on June 15.

The second most important and interesting event is the feast of the Madonna delle Grazie di Montepertuso, on July 2. The choral participation of the inhabitants of this village, fervently devoted to the Madonna, re-evokes through fire and smoke the challenge mentioned earlier between the Madonna and the devil to open a hole through the mountain.

Worth mentioning as well are the feasts of S. Pietro in Laurito and the Madonna del Carmelo in Nocella. In nearly every district the calendar days of the saints,

Previous page:
Procession of Cristo Morto returning to the church

Opposite:
Old photo of Good Friday procession

Below:
Procession of S. Vito

after whom the local church is named, are celebrated.

Easter used to be solemnized with a series of religious processions, introduced by Jesuits into the Kingdom of Naples under Spanish rule, which mirror those celebrated in Spain in the same period, though with a slightly different ritual.

The *Visita ai Sepolcri*, a mystic and fascinating procession of the Holy Week, made up of the hooded from various religious confraternities, clearly goes back to the religious celebrations that the Spaniards brought with them. On Holy Thursday the procession, which began with sacred hymns, went through the streets of Positano, recalling Mary's search for her son. The procession led to every church in town,

where the faithful had prepared the Sepulchre with plants of wheat grown in the dark, and therefore unnaturally white. At the first light of day, on Good Friday, the procession, which grew increasingly large as it went on, arrived in Montepertuso up the steep Tese di S. Giuseppe.

In Piazza Cappella a moving encounter occurred as they met a similar procession from Nocella and walked the last stretch together to the church of the Madonna delle Grazie.

Nowadays, due to the complex problems of traffic and the demise of religious confraternities, this event and that of Christ's death on Good Friday afternoon, designed to rekindle faith and religious unity, have been downsized to a major extent.

Previous page:
On the terrace of Albergo California, by unknown artist
(private collection)

Opposite and below:
Fireworks and the city lighted up on August15, Feast of
the Assunta

Lay feasts

Place of honour must go to Carnival, though this too has lost over the years much of its influence; but, to the joy of children, the procession of masked figures through the streets, with music and dance, has been preserved.

In Montepertuso, up until a few years ago, they put on a farce, *La Zeza*, the parody of certain mishaps of Pulcinella, played by local amateurs who soon fell into the part of Pulcinella, who had no wish to marry his daughter Vincenzella to her suitor don Nicola, or into the part of his wife Zeza, as always of a different opinion, who ordered her poor husband to go and call the bishop to celebrate the wedding. The act ended with Pulcinella inviting the audience to a wedding banquet of dried figs.

Cultural events

Summer sees a host of cultural events. Worth mentioning is *Mare Sole e Cultura*, held in memory of its founders Salvatore and Carlo Attanasio, which takes place in early July in the delightful setting of the cloister of Palazzo Murat, with authors from home and abroad and cultural figures who have distinguished themselves over the past year both nationally and internationally. Since its inception it has increasingly won international critical and public acclaim.

In the same class is the *Rassegna Culturale Domina Positano*, conceived by Angelo Ciaravolo and Roberto Illiano, unique in its being staged from May to October in both Domina Royal Hotel and Poseidon Hotel. The two hotels, with terraces offering panoramic views extending as far as Punta Licosa, feature ample communal facilities, hosting in summertime cultural events of international standing. They are known to attract specialists in the various subjects being presented as well as tourists and laymen.

The *Premio della Danza*, founded in 1969 in honour of Léonide Massine and resolutely supported by Luca Vespoli, head of the Tourist Board for many years, is the traditional event par excellence. Held on the first Saturday of September, it awards prizes to rising national and international stars of ballet. The divine Carla Fracci has been the patron of the event for many years.

The *Musica d'Estate* festival takes place in the same period in the magnificent setting of Palazzo Murat with artists of international fame.

All of the above are organised by the Positalta Association, under the artistic

direction of its president, maestro Luciano Cerroni.

The *Vittorio De Sica Prize*, under the patronage of Emy De Sica, is designed for young film directors.

Cartoons on the Bay, international première of animated films, is held in spring on Spiaggia Grande, also known as Spiagga delle Sirene.

The *Rassegna del Teatro Contemporaneo, Premio Annibale Ruccello*, headed by director Gerardo D'Andrea has been held since 2000. Over the years this event has become internationally popular, attracting many great theatre artists and young hopefuls.

The toil and commitment of associations and individuals alike have borne fruit among the youth of Positano. These include, in the musical arena, pianists Maria Teresa Cinque, Marianna Casola and guitarist Luigi Talamo, very young pupils of the maestro Franco Di Franco, sadly too soon departed, who knew how to instil the passion for music with patience and kindness; maestro Luciano Cerroni and maestro Raimondo di Sandro; soprano Maria Collina, who with Marianna Casola, Luigi Talamo, flautist Maria Gargiulo and guitarist Gianluca Cinque formed the *PosiMuse Ensemble*, famous the world over; Salvatore Cuccaro and other youngsters from Positano who set up the *Young Brass Quintet*; the baroque ensemble *Archè*.

In the theatre the young and promising Pina Irace, Gianmaria Talamo and Giuseppe Rispoli; in classical and modern dance Gioacchino Romano; in the cinema Gianfranco Russo and, for animated film, Ernesto Mandara, the winner of an international prize; for poetry, Rachele Talamo.

Art galleries

The growing importance of Positano in the cultural field is stressed not only by the events described in the previous chapter, but also by the many international art galleries which have sprung up in recent years in the wake of the first art gallery set up in the 1960s by the young Giulio Gargiulo, due to his close ties to artists of the *Art Workshop*, who exhibited their work every summer.

Positano has since become a popular arts centre thanks to the exciting events listed hereunder.

In summer, the Tourist Board used to host exhibitions of national and international artists in its premises, but it wasn't until the 1980s, thanks to Antonio Miniaci, who founded the *Miniaci Art Gallery* (now situated in Via dei Mulini) that a gallery was opened to host and display artists of international fame. What sets it apart from other galleries is that paintings and sculptures are mostly displayed in a garden of orange blossoms, which besides the works of art offers some fine views of Positano.

Idee Arte stands along Viale Pasitea and the *Capri Art Gallery* has its premises in Piazza dei Mulini.

During the summer the Itaca bookshop, the Mediterraneo restaurant, the Pasitea Hotel, the Bar Internazionale at Chiesa Nuova and others play host to art exhibitions and retrospectives of national and international artists who live in Positano. All of these art events have always been successful with both Italian and foreign visitors. To some extent, they also provide support to the idea of establishing a public art gallery in Positano, so as not to lose the heritage of the many artists who have lived and worked here.

GASTRONOMY

Local produce

Local gastronomy is the expression of a dual soul, as it is rooted in the traditions of land and sea. Due to the wild and rugged terrain, the difficulties of transport on land and sea forced local inhabitants to farm for self-sufficiency, cultivating fruits and vegetables suitable to be preserved for fairly long periods. Rearing cattle, dairy cows in particular, pigs and farmyard animals, was to provide the necessary protein.

Almost every home had an oven for baking bread (some well-preserved ovens may be seen in 18th-century villas) and an orchard for family needs.

Chestnuts, gathered in the rich groves of the Monti Lattari, and in particular in the woods of S. Maria del Castello, were also ground for flour, with a special kind of bread was made, called *pane italico* by the Germans, enriched, on special occasions, with currents, pine-nuts, walnuts and dried fruits.

In recent years chocolate was added to make the sweet *castagnaccio* pie. The *zeppola* belongs to tradition: to this delicious doughnut the end of year festival, as mentioned earlier, is dedicated.

Contact with other Mediterranean peoples left its mark on local cuisine. From the east arrived spices, fine pepper and other essences, impossible to obtain from other sources, which flavoured local food and helped to preserve cured meats (every single family would have at least one

375

pig for winter reserves of meat, lard and dripping) and various species of fruit and vegetables. Worth noting in particular is the lemon, which has become a symbol, almost, of the Amalfi Coast and is used for the special liqueur, *limoncello*, and the eggplant, which besides being prepared in various ways for winter preserves, gave rise to the special eggplant bake, the *parmigiana*, blending perfectly with mozzarella cheese.

Social changes have seen the demise of many of the local products, no longer competitive or remunerative.

As well as the traditional abundant production of fresh meats, cured meats, cheeses, wines and oils, excellent products are available from nearby towns (Agerola, Vico Equense), from the plain of Paestum and the Cilento area, with which Positano has always enjoyed a close relationship, both commercially and culturally.

Famous restaurants and local dishes

The need to satisfy the demands of cosmopolitan tourists and guests, increasingly drawn by arts and local culinary tradition, has led to a modern elaboration of many recipes of the past. Fortune has smiled on clever restaurateurs, masters in adapting simple Mediterranean dishes to these new demands with respect for tradition.

The simple tomato salad with slices of mozzarella cheese, seasoned with origano and basil, yielded the *caprese*; fresh anchovies were marinated for extra flavour; fried shortfin squid, traditionally prepared on the Feast of the Assumption, have now become an integral part of the fried mixed-fish dish, *fritto misto*.

Many restaurants have diligently adapted dishes of the past, all along keeping unchanged several traditional dishes and sweets. Among these, pride of place goes to the famous Buca di Bacco Restaurant, formerly the Flavio Gioia coffeehouse, the first restaurant in Positano, considered since its birth in the early 1900s a meeting place for artists and important local figures. In 1952 a Scandinavian poet, between one drink and another, renamed it "Buca di Bacco", which pleased the owner.

The restaurant has been able to preserve traditional local cuisine, thanks largely to the Rispoli family, who founded and maintained it, emphasizing certain peculiar features such as the very special chestnut

cake, reworked by housekeeper Anna Rispoli.

Another restaurant responsible for the preservation and reappraisal of traditional local cuisine is Chez Black, the old "Da Peppino" patisserie, famous in the past for the assortment and quality of its dishes, sweets and ice creams. One of the striking features of this restaurant is that practically every year it designs a new speciality, such as spaghetti with sea urchins' sauce, which was deservedly successful.

Le Tre Sorelle, originally a pizzeria founded by three sisters, Adelina, Anna and Giovanna, in the 1950s, is the other famous restaurant of Positano. The heirs to the sisters faithfully preserved tradition and

quality. Il Caporale is known for its home-made dishes and seafood.

The Covo dei Saraceni, whose terrace overlooks the whole beach, serves up local and international specialities.

La Cambusa, the waterside restaurant, has become famous for its seafood specialities, and not only for them.

At the Incanto, a new, fascinating complex carved out of ancient caves and expansion of former open terracing, a delightful restaurant, Le Terrazze, has brought back into vogue the Roman fish sauce *garum*, now produced in nearby Cetara, along with *bottarga* fish roe, an Arab product introduced in the Middle Ages by local traders.

Adjoining the Palazzo Murat Hotel is Al Palazzo restaurant. Near the beach of Fornillo is Da Pupetto, another typical restaurant of Positano, belonging to the hotel of the same name, managed by the Celentano brothers, who have made a warm welcome and Mediterranean cuisine their byword.

Other restaurants worthy of note are Lo Guarracino in Via Positanesi d'America, Il Grottino Azzurro at Chiesa Nuova and Da Costantino, Da Bruno and Il Canneto around the town.

At Fornillo stand the Mediterraneo and Il Capitano, which promote typical regional products; Next 2 Light Dinner, Il Fornillo, Il Saraceno d'Oro and Da Vincenzo. Near the Piazzetta dei Mulini are Max and the restaurant-pizzeria Valle dei Mulini.

On the beach of Laurito are Da Adolfo and Le Sirene, belonging to the hotel of the same name, with La Taverna del Leone along the road to Amalfi.

At Montepertuso are three excellent restaurants: Donna Rosa, Il Ritrovo and La Tagliata.

At Nocella is the Santa Croce inn with its typical country cuisine.

Bibliography

Afeltra G. - Buzzati D., *Positano darà la luce al mondo*, Cava de' Tirreni 1994.

Albore Livadie C., *Positano: La grotta La Porta*, in *Archeologia a Piano di Sorrento*, Piano di Sorrento 1990.

Alessandro G., *Coste porti e approdi della Campania*, Genova 1974.

Alfani G., *La cultura del limone nella costiera amalfitana*, "Il Follaro" 1974.

Almagià R., *L'opera geografica di Luca Holstenio*, Città del Vaticano 1942.

Amari M., *Storia dei Musulmani in Sicilia*, Catania 1939.

Amos, P. - Gambardella A., *Il paesaggio naturale-agrario della costa amalfitana*, Salerno 1976.

Andres S., *Positano. Storie di una città sul mare*, Amalfi 1991.

Apuzzo A., *L'invenzione della bussola e Flavio Gioia*, Napoli 1964.

Bacchelli R., *Italia per terra e per mare*, Milano 1927.

Barra F., *La Costa d'Amalfi nell'età moderna. Economia e società*, in *La costa di Amalfi nel secolo XVII*, Amalfi 2002.

Benvenuti G., *Storia della Repubblica di Amalfi*, Pisa 1985.

Benvenuti G., *Le Repubbliche marinare - Amalfi, Pisa, Genova e Venezia*, Roma 2005.

Bignardi M. (a cura di), *Ivan Zagoruiko, I pittori russi a Positano*, Exhibition Catalogue, Ravello 1995.

Bignardi M. (a cura di), *Positano nell'immaginario di un secolo*, Salerno 2000.

Bonuccelli G., *Industria mesolitica della Grotta Erica di Positano*, "Rivista di Scienze Preistoriche", 26, 1971, pp. 347-372.

Bracco V., *Le urne romane della Costa d'Amalfi*, Salerno 1977.

Bracco V., *Inscriptiones Italiae, vol. I, Regio I, Fasc. I, Salernum*, Roma 1981.

Braudel F., *Civiltà e Imperi del Mediterraneo nell'età di Filippo II*, Torino 1976.

Broccoli U., *Cronache militari e marittime del Golfo di Napoli*, Roma 1953.

Camera M., *Istoria della città e costiera di Amalfi*, Salerno 1836.

Camera M., *Memorie storico-diplomatiche dell'antica città e ducato di Amalfi*, Salerno 1881.

Camera M., *Scritti minori inediti e rari*, Castellammare di Stabia 1994.

Camardo D. - Esposito M., *Le frontiere di Amalfi*, Castellammare di Stabia 1995.

Camelia G. (a cura di), *Paesaggi dell'anima tra cattedrali di roccia. Metamorfosi dell'immagine della Costa d'Amalfi fra incanto e maniera*, Amalfi 2005.

Caputo G., *Flora e vegetazione delle Isole "Li Galli" (Golfo di Salerno)*, "Delpinoa" 1964, pp. 29-54.

Celentano A. R., *La chiesa di Santa Maria di Positano*, Maiori 2005.

Cinque S., *Per l'inaugurazione della luce elettrica a Montepertuso, 1° luglio 1939*, Amalfi 1939.

Citarella A. O., *Il commercio di Amalfi nell'alto Medioevo*, Salerno 1977.

Cito di Torrecuso R., *Positano. Ricordi ed impressioni*, Napoli 1924.

Colombi P. G., *Da Montepertuso a Nocella*, "Le vie d'Italia", 58, 1942, pp. 86-89.

Criscuolo V., *Le pergamene dell'Archivio della Collegiata di Maiori*, Amalfi 2003.

Della Corte M., *L'origine del nome di Positano*, Salerno 1937.

-- "Diario (Il) di Positano" mensile pubblicato a Positano dal 1965 al 1970.

Di Giacomo L., *Positano medioevale*, Salerno 1986.

Douglas N., *La terra delle Sirene*, Varese 1991.

-- "Duca (Il)", mensile pubblicato a Positano dal 1989 al 2002.

Ercolino R., *Le torri di guardia nel ducato di Amalfi*, Salerno 1974.

Ercolino R., *Mohamed Essad Bey: il musulmano di Positano*, "Il Duca", Positano 1990.

Ercolino R., Il sistema difensivo di Massalubrense, in *I Beni Culturali di Massa Lubrense*, Castellammare di Stabia 1992.

Ercolino R., *La frontiera di Mare*, in *Enciclopedia del Mezzogiorno*, Napoli 1996.

Ercolino R., *L'Isola delle Sirene "Li Galli"*, Castellammare di Stabia 1997.

Ercolino R., *Fortificazioni alla Marina*, in *La Lobra, culla della città di Massa Lubrense*, Castellammare di Stabia 2000, pp. 205-213.

Ercolino R., *La produzione della calce nella Penisola sorrentino-amalfitana*, in *Le arti dell'acqua e del fuoco*, Amalfi 2004, pp. 215-261.

-- *Fatto e ragioni dell'Università della terra di Positano contro l'Ill. Marchese della medesima terra* (Archivio della Badia di Cava de' Tirreni, Fondo Mansi).

Ferraro S., *Nocelle: un borgo silenzioso e ridente*, "La Riviera", Napoli, 15 Novembre 1978.

Ferraro S., *Un'urna romana a Nocelle di Positano*, "Rivista ecclesiastica dell'archidiocesi di Amalfi e della diocesi di Cava dei Tirreni", 57, 1978, pp. 214-217.

Ferraro S., *Un'urna romana a Nocelle, una frazione di Positano*, "Il Gazzettino Vesuviano" 8, 14, 1978.

Fiengo G. - Abbate G., *Le case a volta della Costa di Amalfi*, Amalfi 2001.

Gabrieli F. - Scerrato U., *Gli Arabi in Italia*, Milano 1979.

Galanti G. M., *Della descrizione geografica e politica delle Sicilie*, Napoli 1790.

Galasso G., *Le città campane nell'Alto Medioevo*, in *Mezzogiorno medioevale e moderno*, Torino 1965, pp. 61-135.

Gargano G., *La bussola e Flavio Gioia, Il mistero dell'invenzione che sconvolse le tecniche della navigazione*, Salerno 2006.

Gargiulo G., *Viaggio nel cuore della Rudolflandia*, "Il Mattino", 27 July 1994.

Gay I., *L'Italia meridionale e l'impero bizantino*, Firenze 1917.

Guadagno M., *La vegetazione della Penisola Sorrentina*, "Bullettino dell'Orto Botanico dell'Università di Napoli", 5, 1916.

Guarino D., *Chiesa di Santa Maria Assunta di Positano: restauro e musealizzazione delle cripte del campanile*, "Apollo", 21, 2005, pp. 143-157.

Guendalina G., *Il limone e la Costa di Amalfi*, Maiori 2001.

Guerritore A., *Gli stemmi civici dell'antica Repubblica amalfitana*, Roma 1920.

Hatzelf (von) A., *Positano*, Freiburg 1925.

Hellersberg M., *Positano zum seine Geschichte*, Napoli 1955.

Imperato G., *Amalfi nella natura, nella storia nell'arte*, Amalfi 1955 (reprinted 1967).

-- *Itinerari salernitani, I sentieri dello spirito*, Club Alpino Italiano, Napoli 2000.

Knight C., *Essad Bey a Positano*, "Rass. del Centro di Cultura e Storia Amalfitana", n. 6, 1993, pp. 135-142.

Knight C., *La torre di Clavel*, Capri 1999.

Knight C., *Mikhail Nikolaevich Semenov, positanese d'adozione*, "Rassegna del Centro di Cultura e Storia Amalfitana", n. 11-12, 1996, pp. 243-265.

La Capria R., *Ultimi viaggi nell'Italia perduta*, Cava de' Tirreni 1999.

Laurenzi C., *Sono bastati trent'anni per distruggere Positano*, "Corriere della Sera", 8 April 1962.

Lipinsky A. e L., *Il tesoro sacro della Costiera amalfitana*, Amalfi 1989.

Lomax A. - Carpitella D., *Folklore musicale italiano*, 1973.

Mafroni G., *Storia della marina italiana*, Livorno 1899.

Maiuri A., *La straordinaria scoperta di un macellaio di Positano*, "Corriere della Sera", 25 October 1954.

Maiuri A., *Passeggiate sorrentine*, Ercolano 1990.

Massine L., *My Life in Ballett*, Londra 1968.

Mattiello A., Boalim, pirata saraceno e Capri, in *Capri e l'Islam*, Capri 2002.

Menichetti G., *Il Porto, storia di un canyon selvaggio*, Maiori 2003.

Mertens R., *Le lucertole delle isole del Golfo di Salerno*, Senckenberg 1960

Micciché A., *Positano. La gemma della divina costiera*, "Le vie d'Italia", 48, 1941, pp. 1056-1063.

Mingazzini P. - Pfister F., *Forma Italiae, Regio I, Latium et Campania, Surrentum*, Firenze 1946.

Mingazzini P. - Pfister F., *Positano. Resti di una villa romana presso la marina*, "Notizie degli scavi di antichità", Roma 1931, pp. 356-359.

Monti G. M., *Il Mezzogiorno d'Italia nel Medioevo*, Bari 1930.

Monti G. M., *Il commercio marittimo di Amalfi fuori d'Italia*, Roma 1940.

Montuori F., *Per la festività della solenne coronazione di S. Maria di Positano celebrata nel dì 15 agosto dell'anno 1789 coll'aggiunta di nuove grazie compartite ai suoi devoti*, Napoli 1815 (reprint: Salerno 1985).

Moretti G., *La prima repubblica marinara d'Italia*, Ravenna 1914.

Norwich J. J., *I Normanni nel sud*, Milano 1971.

Napei M., *Positano*, voce in *Enciclopedia dell'arte antica*, Roma 1965.

Napolitano G. G., *Il patriarca russo di Positano*, "L'Illustrazione italiana", January 1951.

Pane R., *La cascata di Caserta e la cascatella di Positano*, "Napoli Nobilissima", fasc. 5, 1979, pp. 199-200.

Panetta R., *I Saraceni in Italia*, Milano 1973.

Pansa F., *Istoria dell'antica Repubblica d'Amalfi*, Napoli 1724.

Parlato A., *Flavio Gioia e la bussola di Positano*, Napoli 2005.

Parlato A., *Ulisse e le sirene di Positano*, Napoli 2006.

Parrilli M., *Da Positano a Palinuro*, Salerno 1959.

Pasanisi O., *La costruzione delle torri marittime ordinate dalla Regia Corte di Napoli*, Napoli 1926.

Patti O., *Morfogenesi di due cavità in costiera amalfitana: la grotta Mirabella e la grotta del Capriglione (Positano)*, "Annuario Speleologico", Club Alpino Italiano di Napoli, Napoli 1976-77.

Pecora A., *I porti minori della Campania, della Calabria e della Venezia*, Napoli 1954.

Pietroiusti M., *Positano realtà e sogno*, Milano 1990.

Pittari C., *Positano è. Storia, tradizioni e immagini*, Napoli 1986.

Proto V. (a cura di), *La costa delle sirene. Tra Vietri, Ravello, Amalfi e Positano, 1850-1950*, Napoli 1992.

Radmilli A. M. - Tongiorgi M., *Gli scavi nella grotta La Porta di Positano. Contributo alla conoscenza del Mesolitico italiano*, "Rivista di Scienze Preistoriche" 1959, pp. 91-109.

Ralli G., *Sulla costa di Positano. Torre d'artista*, "Casa Vogue", Milano, n. 154, 1984, pp. 88-95

Richter D. (a cura di), *Alla ricerca del Sud. Tre secoli di viaggi ad Amalfi nell'immaginario europeo*, Amalfi 1989.

Richter D. - Romito M. - Talalay M., *In fuga dalla storia. Esuli dai totalitarismi del Novecento sulla Costa d'Amalfi*, Catalogo della Mostra, Amalfi 2005.

Rispoli G., *Positano "ieri e oggi"*, Verona 1982.

Rispoli V., *Positanerie*, Sorrento 1979.

Rizzi Zannoni G. A., *Atlante geografico del Regno di Napoli*, Catanzaro 1993 (reprint).

Romito M., *Dodici secoli di documentazione archeologica in una mostra a Positano*, "Rassegna Storica Salernitana", 6, 1986, pp. 265-266.

Romito M., *Tasselli di storia a Positano*, Salerno 1998.

Romito M., *Stefan Andres a Positano - Uno scrittore, un artista ai margini del mondo (1937-1949)*, Salerno 2002.

Rossi A. - Radmilli A. M., *Ricerche preistoriche a Positano*, "Bollettino della Società Paleontologica Italiana.", 65, 1956.

Russo F., *La difesa costiera nel Regno di Napoli dal XVI al XIX secolo*, Roma 1989.

Russo F., *Trenta secoli di fortificazioni in Campania*, Piedimonte Matese 1999.

Russo F., *Le torri anticorsare vicereali con particolare riferimento a quelle della costa campana*, Piedimonte Matese 2001.

Schiavo A., *Monumenti della costa di Amalfi*, Milano 1941.

Semenoff M. N., *Bacco e Sirene*, Milano 1942.

Semenoff M. N., *Mulino d'Arienzo - Memorie di un pescatore* "Il Giornale", nn. 244 e 286, 1951.

Sereni E., *Storia del paesaggio agrario*, Torino 1952.

Steinbeck J., *Positano*, Salerno 1955.

Talamo E., *Monografia della città di Positano*, Napoli 1890 (reprint: Atrani 1984).

Talamo E., *Storia del simulacro della Madonna di Positano*, Portici 1905.

Testa A., *Positano e la danza nel mondo*, Roma 2002.

Testa A., *Uno sguardo indietro e ai margini della danza*, Anzio 2006.

Tongiorgi E. - Radmilli A. M., *Gli scavi nella grotta La Porta a Positano ed il Mesolitico italiano*, "Bollettino di Paleontologia Italiana", 66, 1957.

Toschi P. - Penna R., *Le tavolette votive della Madonna dell'Arco*, Cava dei Tirreni 1971.

Verde M., *Un documento inedito per la storia di Positano: il patto di amicizia con l'Università di Vico Equense del 14 luglio 1501*, "Rassegna del Centro di Cultura e Storia Amalfitana", 4, 1992, pp. 101-104.

Verde M., *Un inedito documento sui possedimenti positanesi in Vico Equense*, "Rassegna del Centro di Cultura e Storia Amalfitana", 14, 1997, pp. 269-277.

Verde M., *Viaggio da Vietri a Positano. Da una "Memoria" del 1858 degli avvocati Leopoldo Tarantini e Nicola Amore*, "Rassegna del Centro di Cultura e Storia Amalfitana", 23-24, 2002, pp. 233-238.

Verrastro V., *Il monastero ed il santuario di S. Maria e S. Vito di Positano nelle fonti archivistiche della Basilicata* (under press).

Vespoli G., *Storia di Positano*, Amalfi 1971.

Vespoli L., *Le lacrime del silenzio*, Maiori 1996.

Viola G. C., *Aria di Positano*, "Bellezza" 1992.

Visetti G., *Le coste di Sorrento e di Amalfi*, Ercolano 1991.

Woude, van der, J., *Spel in Positano*, Gravenhage 1937.

CONTENTS